MAKERS
of the
MUSLIM
WORLD

Elijah Muhammad

TITLES IN THE MAKERS OF THE MUSLIM WORLD SERIES

Series Editor: Patricia Crone, Institute for Advanced Study, Princeton

Abd al-Ghani al-Nabulusi, Samer Akkach
'Abd al-Malik, Chase F. Robinson
Abd al-Rahman III, Maribel Fierro
Abu Nuwas, Philip Kennedy
Ahmad al-Mansur, Mercedes García-Arenal
Ahmad ibn Hanbal, Christopher Melchert
Ahmad Riza Khan Barelwi, Usha Sanyal
Akbar, André Wink
Al-Ma'mun, Michael Cooperson
Al-Mutanabbi, Margaret Larkin
Amir Khusraw, Sunil Sharma
Ashraf 'Ali Thanawi, Muhammad Qasim Zaman
Chinggis Khan, Michal Biran
El Hajj Beshir Agha, Jane Hathaway
Fazlallah Astarabadi and the Hurufis, Shazad Bashir
Ghazali, Eric Ormsby
Hasan al-Banna, Gudrun Krämer
Husain Ahmad Madani, Barbara Metcalf
Ibn 'Arabi, William C. Chittick
Ibn Fudi, Ahmad Dallal
Ikhwan al-Safa, Godefroid de Callatay
Imam Shafi'i, Kecia Ali
Karim Khan Zand, John R. Perry
Mehmed Ali, Khaled Fahmy
Mu'awiya ibn abi Sufyan, R. Stephen Humphreys
Muhammad Abduh, Mark Sedgwick
Mulla Sadra, Sayeh Meisami
Nasser, Joel Gordon
Nazira Zeineddine, Miriam Cooke
Sa'di, Homa Katouzian
Shaykh Mufid, Tamima Bayhom-Daou
Usama ibn Munqidh, Paul M. Cobb

For current information and details of other books in the series, please visit www.oneworld-publications.com

MAKERS
of the
MUSLIM
WORLD

Elijah Muhammad

HERBERT BERG

ONEWORLD

ELIJAH MUHAMMAD

A Oneworld Book
Published by Oneworld Publications 2013

A CIP record for this title is available
from the British Library

ISBN 978–1–85168–803–6
eISBN 978–1–78074–330–1

Typeset by Jayvee, Trivandrum, India
Printed and bound in CPI Anthony Rowe, UK

Oneworld Publications
10 Bloomsbury Street,
London WC1B 3SR, England

CONTENTS

Preface vii
Acknowledgments viii
Main Persons and Technical Terms ix
Chronology xii

INTRODUCTION 1

1 **ISLAM AND AFRICAN AMERICANS** 7
African American Muslim slaves and African American religion 7
Ahmadis and the Moorish Science Temple 13
Wali Fard Muhammad 19
Wallace D. Ford 19
Detroit's Allah 20

2 **ELIJAH POOLE** 25
Racism in the South 25
Racism in the North 29
The Nation of Islam 30

3 **THE APOSTLE OF ALLAH** 35
A decade of persecution, preaching and prison 35
Two decades of success 38
A decade of decline 46

4 **BLACK ISLAM** 49
The rise and fall of the white race 52
The five principles of Islam 54
Allah and Allahs 54
Black angels and white devils 57
Black prophets 58

Glorious, poisonous, and future books 64
The Last Day and the Fall of America 68
The five pillars of Islam 70
Shahada 70
Salat 71
Sawm 74
Zakat 75
Hajj 76
Dietary regulations 77

5 WHAT MUSLIMS BELIEVE AND WHAT MUSLIMS WANT 81
Do for self: economic self-sufficiency 87
A land of our own: separation, not integration 90
Protect your women! 93
Be yourself! Black pride 96

6 THE TEXTUAL SOURCES OF ISLAM 103
The Sira 103
The Sunna 106
The Qur'an 107

7 OTHER MUSLIMS 115
Hypocrites 116
American Muslim opposition 120
"Copper-colored" brothers 123
White Muslims 127
Islamic trajectories 130
Warith Deen Mohammed 131
Louis Farrakhan 138

CONCLUSION: THE LEGACIES 143

Further Reading 151
Bibliography 153
Index 157

PREFACE

Elijah Muhammad tends to be neglected by scholars of Islam. Their lack of interest often reflects the conviction shared by many Muslims that he and his followers should not be considered Muslims. Alternatively, his Nation of Islam is seen simply as a short-lived American aberration of Islam, a product of the now fading racial tensions in the United States. Thus, only a few American historians of race need to study him and even fewer sociologists need to analyze his movement. Elijah Muhammad also suffers from having been eclipsed in celebrity by his followers: Malcolm X, Warith Deen Mohammed, and Louis Farrakhan. However, each of them stands on the shoulders of Elijah Muhammad, the man who converted them to Islam. Scholars of Islam should not therefore ignore him, for he and his followers saw themselves first and foremost as Muslims or black Muslims, not Muslim blacks.

The more pertinent issue is whether he can be considered a "Maker of the Muslim World" and thus merit the attention this book gives him. My hope is that by the end of this book, the reader will come away with two conclusions. One, Elijah Muhammad has a unique and most intriguing perspective on Islam, and to understand why he formulated it in the particular (even peculiar) way that he did, one has to understand his context. Two, he almost single-handedly developed an indigenous form of Islam in the United States. This is something that no other person calling himself or herself a Muslim has been able to do. More effectively than the millions of Muslim immigrants to the United States, he made the United States part of the Muslim world, at least in the eyes of millions of African Americans. He is, therefore, a maker of the Muslim world.

ACKNOWLEDGMENTS

I wish to thank Sarah E. Rollens for reading a draft of this book and giving me many valuable suggestions that led to significant improvements. I would also like to thank Matt Eshleman, who many times allowed me to ramble on about Elijah Muhammad and thereby helped me formulate my thoughts. Their time, encouragement, glasses of excellent wine, and friendship made this book and much else possible.

MAIN PERSONS AND TECHNICAL TERMS

Ahmadis An Islamic reform movement from British India that sent missionaries to the United States in the early twentieth century and is the source of Elijah Muhammad's translation of the Qur'an.

Ali, Muhammad An Olympic gold medalist and World Heavyweight Champion in boxing who converted to the Nation of Islam. Also known as Cassius Clay, Jr.

Ali, Maulana Muhammad The leader of the Lahori Ahmadiyya movement whose English translation of the Qur'an was favored by Elijah Muhammad (d. 1951).

Batini An often pejorative description for finding esoteric meanings in the Qur'an underlying the more obvious meanings.

Circle Seven Koran The common name of *The Holy Koran of the Moorish Science Temple*, the scripture produced by Drew Ali.

Civil war The civil war (1861–65) between the United States of America (the Union) and the Confederate States of America (the Confederacy) comprised of the eleven Southern states that seceded. The victory of the Union forces led to the abolition of slavery.

Drew Ali, Noble Founder of the Moorish Science Temple of America, Inc. Also known as Timothy Drew and Sharif Abdul Ali (d. 1929).

Druze A religion that considers the Fatimid caliph al-Hakim (d. or disappeared in 1021) to be an incarnation of Allah.

Fard Muhammad, Wali Founder of the Nation of Islam and thought by Elijah Muhammad to be Allah. The F.B.I. identified him as Wallace D. Ford.

Farrakhan, Louis Elijah Muhammad's National Representative and after 1977 the leader of a resurrected Nation of Islam. Also known as Louis E. Walcott and Louis X (b. 1933).

F.B.I. Federal Bureau of Investigation whose purview includes domestic intelligence and federal criminal investigations.

Fruit of Islam The male self-defense force of the Nation of Islam.

Garvey, Marcus Founder of the Universal Negro Improvement Association that advocated global pan-Africanism and economic empowerment (d. 1940).

Ghulat A term used by heresiographers to describe those Shi'ites whom others view as going to extremes in matters of religion, particularly by deifying particular humans.

Lynchings Extrajudicial executions by hanging of African Americans particularly in the post-civil war South.

Maliki One of the four prominent schools of Islamic law within Sunni Islam.

Mirza Ghulam Ahmad Founder of the Ahmadiyya Muslim Community who claimed to be the Mahdi and the Second Coming of Christ (d. 1908).

Mohammed, Warith Deen Son of Elijah Muhammad who led and transformed the Nation of Islam after his father's death in 1975. Originally named Wallace D. Muhammad (d. 2008).

Muhammad, Akbar Son of Elijah Muhammad who studied at al-Azhar in Egypt.

Muhammad, Clara Wife of Elijah Muhammad (d. 1972).

Muhammad, Elijah Leader of the Nation of Islam from 1934 to 1975. Also known as Elijah Poole and Elijah Karriem (d. 1975).

Muhammad, (Jabir) Herbert Son of Elijah Muhammad and editor of *Muhammad Speaks* (d. 2008).

Muhammad Speaks Newspaper of the Nation of Islam.

Saviour's Day An annual rally or convention of the Nation of Islam celebrating the birth of Fard Muhammad on 26 February.

Sharrieff, Raymond Long-time Supreme Captain of the Fruit of Islam.

The South States in the southeastern and south central United States of America that were part of the Confederacy during the civil war.

The Tribe of Shabazz An ancient black civilization originally from Mecca and Egypt, but a group of which moved to central Africa and became the ancestors of African Americans.

University of Islam The Nation of Islam's schools for children from kindergarten to high school.

X, Malcolm National Minister of the Nation of Islam until he left the organization in 1964. Also known as El-Hajj Malik El-Shabazz and Malcolm Little (d. 1965).

Yakub The evil black scientist whose eugenics program created the white race.

CHRONOLOGY

1527 Estavan, the first African American Muslim, comes to North America.

1619 First African slaves brought to the English colony of Virginia.

1865 End of the American Civil War and slavery in the United States.

1877 Birth of Wali Fard Muhammad in Mecca.

1886 Birth of Timothy Drew (Noble Drew Ali) in North Carolina.

1891 Birth of Wallace D. Ford.

1893 American Moslem Brotherhood founded in New York City by Russell Alexander Webb.

1897 Birth of Elijah Poole.

1913 Wallace D. Ford thought to have immigrated to the United States.

1913 Drew Ali founds the Canaanite Temple in Newark, New Jersey.

1914 The prophesied end of devils' rule, extended in order to save the Lost-Found Nation of Islam in the wilderness of North America.

1919 Elijah Poole marries Clara Evans.

1920 The Ahmadiyya missionary Mufti Muhammad Sadiq arrives in the United States.

1923 Elijah Poole moves to Detroit.

1925 Birth of Malcolm Little.

1927 Drew Ali publishes his *Circle Seven Koran*.

1928 Drew Ali founds the Moorish Science Temple of America, Inc.

1929 Drew Ali dies.

1930 Wali Fard Muhammad arrives from Arabia to the United States on 4 July to begin his mission.

1931 Elijah Poole meets Fard Muhammad.

1933 Fard Muhammad is expelled from Detroit and moves to Chicago.

1934 Elijah Muhammad sees Fard Muhammad for the last time in Chicago.

1935 Elijah Muhammad leaves Detroit for Chicago.

1942 Elijah Muhammad arrested and imprisoned for dodging the draft.

1946 Elijah Muhammad released from prison.

1952 Malcolm Little meets Elijah Muhammad and is renamed Malcolm X.

1959 Elijah Muhammad makes his *'umra* and visits countries in the Middle East and Pakistan.

1964 Malcolm X leaves the Nation of Islam.

1965 Malcolm X is assassinated.

1975 Elijah Muhammad dies, and his son Wallace D. Muhammad (later, Warith Deen Mohammed) acclaimed the Supreme Minister of the Nation of Islam.

1977 Louis Farrakhan resurrects the Nation of Islam under his leadership.

2008 Warith Deen Mohammed dies.

INTRODUCTION

> 1. Who made the Holy Koran or Bible? How long ago? Will you tell us why does Islam re-new her history every twenty-five thousand years?
>
> Ans. – The Holy Koran or Bible is made by the original people, who is Allah, the supreme being, or (black man) of Asia; the Koran will expire in the year twenty-five thousand. Nine thousand and eight years from the date of this writing the Nation of Islam is all wise and does everything right and exact. The planet Earth, which is the home of Islam and is approximately twenty-five thousand miles in circumference, so the wise man of the East (black man) makes history or Koran, to equal his home circumference, a year to every mile and thus evertime his history lasts twenty-five thousand years, he re-news it for another twenty-five thousand years.
>
> (F.B.I. file 105-63642)

On 20 February 1934, Wali Fard Muhammad, then simply referred to as "our Prophet, W. D. Fard," asked one of his ministers, Elijah Muhammad, forty questions. "Lesson #2," the pamphlet that contained these questions and answers, would serve as the Nation of Islam's main literature until Elijah Muhammad began writing his columns and booklets in the late 1950s. Although the answer to the first question quoted above mentions the Qur'an, Islam, and Allah, little else in it is recognizably "Islamic."

Questions two through eight ask about the world's size, physical features, and weather. Then the subject turns to God and the devil: "Why does the devil teach the eight[y]-five per cent, that a mystery God brings all this [that is, the world]?" and "Who is that mystery God?" Elijah Muhammad answers that the belief in an invisible God permits the devils to enslave the eighty-five percent. In subsequent answers Elijah Muhammad explains that his people have been lost for 379 years, during which time they were enslaved, beaten, and killed by those who taught them to worship this mystery God. But now the Son of man, the Prophet W. D. Fard, has come to remedy that situation and along with his five percent who are righteous teachers to teach "who the living God is and teach that the living God is the Son of man, the supreme being, the black man of Asia; and teach Freedom, Justice, and Equality to all the human family of the planet Earth, otherwise known as civilized people. Also [a]s Moslem and Moslem Sons." The devil was created some six thousand years ago by a great black scientist, a Mr. Yakub, born some twenty miles from Mecca. He "grafted" this devil from his own black people through selective breeding over a six-hundred-year period. The result was a weak, wicked, and *white* race who cannot be reformed, but whose prophesied destruction is imminent, thus demonstrating the power and reality of this human and black Allah.

The questions themselves are odd, but it is the answers that most Muslims find to be heretical. Yet Elijah Muhammad and his followers in the Lost-Found Nation of Islam in the wilderness of North America, or just "Nation of Islam," prayed to Allah, fasted, identified themselves as Muslims, and read the Qur'an. Over two decades later, when the Federal Bureau of Investigation (F.B.I.) asked Elijah Muhammad what credentials Fard Muhammad, then referred to as Allah, had given his messenger, he simply replied: the Holy Qur'an.

Elijah Muhammad is a fascinating Muslim figure not only because he (re)introduced Islam into the United States and was by far Islam's most successful missionary there, but also because his formulation of Islam forces Muslims and scholars to reevaluate their often normative definitions of this religious tradition. To dismiss the Nation of Islam as un-Islamic, or worse, to ridicule the teachings of Elijah Muhammad, is to discount his tremendous impact on Islam in the United States in general and on African Americans in particular.

In the mid-1930s, Elijah Muhammad was just one of several competing leaders of the embryonic movement begun by the mysterious Wali Fard Muhammad, who claimed to be a prophet of Islam and who had recently disappeared. By the time of his death in 1975, Elijah Muhammad led a movement that may have numbered a few hundred thousand, making him the most powerful Muslim in the United States of America. Even before his death he was overshadowed by the growing legend of Malcolm X, and after his death by the activities of Louis Farrakhan and his own son Warith Deen Mohammed (formerly known as Wallace D. Muhammad). Each of these men, however, was brought to Islam by Elijah Muhammad. And although Malcolm X and Elijah Muhammad's son came to reject his idiosyncratic and racial formulation of Islam, Elijah Muhammad was responsible for introducing hundreds of thousands, perhaps even millions, of African Americans to Islam. Almost four decades after his death, he remains by far the most influential American Muslim.

Many other Muslims, however, object to that description; they are unwilling to believe he was a real Muslim. Elijah Muhammad's personal commitment to Allah and his emphasis on the Qur'an are not in dispute. He certainly called himself a Muslim and his religion he consistently referred to as Islam. The problem lies primarily with his claim that Wali Fard Muhammad was "Allah in person," that he himself was his messenger, that heaven and hell were here on Earth, and that the white man was the devil. These teachings contradict some of the basic teachings of Islam as traditionally formulated, and so many Muslims outside the Nation of Islam vehemently object to the description of Elijah Muhammad as a "Muslim" and his movement as "Islam."

From at least the time of the death of Muhammad (b. 'Abd Allah in 632 C.E.) Muslims have been divided on the doctrines, practices, and polity of the religion he espoused. Certainly subsequent history has shown that it is far better to speak of Islams or formulations of Islam. It would be fruitless for a scholar to search for a continuous essence that extends from Muhammad to all people who identify themselves as Muslims and that somehow links all of these formulations of Islam. Nor is it the function of the scholar to construct a normative Islam by which these formulations can be judged. Thus, though Elijah Muhammad's often tense relationship with other Muslims will be explored, the point is not to determine if he was a "real Muslim." More interesting questions to be explored include: why did Elijah Muhammad's Islam take the form that it did? Why was his message so powerful and attractive to so many African Americans? How did Elijah Muhammad understand the major practices and beliefs of Islam, and how did he justify them using the Qur'an? What was the relationship between himself and non-Nation of Islam Muslims? And what was his legacy? That is to say, why does he qualify as a maker of the Muslim world?

By answering these questions, it will become obvious that Elijah Muhammad came from a context that few if any Muslims before him had experienced, which then led him to formulate an Islam that contemporary Muslims could not have foreseen. As unique or deviant as his Islam may appear, through it he was able to do what no other Muslim missionary has succeeded in doing: to convert a large number of Americans to a religion that at the time was almost completely foreign to American soil. And he did so in the face of strong and sustained opposition. By the end of his life there were mosques in almost every major city, and Islam was no longer a religion merely of immigrants and their descendants. He had established a foothold for Islam in the United States.

Yet another way of framing Elijah Muhammad within a larger Islamic context is to compare his teaching with those of the ghulat, a term used by heresiographers to accuse Muslims of exaggeration or hyperbole (ghuluw) in religious matters. It was employed (often by Shi'is against rival Shi'is) to disapprove of exalting the imams above ordinary humans, for example by suggesting that Ali did not die or that he was an incarnation of Allah. Elijah Muhammad was very much outside of this sectarian milieu, but three characteristics of ghuluw have parallels in his teachings. First, some of the ghulat are accused of teaching that Allah incarnates in the bodies of the imams. For Elijah Muhammad, Fard Muhammad is Allah. Second, some of the ghulat reject that the Shari'a, Islamic law, is obligatory. Elijah Muhammad rarely even referred to the Shari'a. Third, some of the ghulat saw hidden, symbolic meanings in the Qur'an. Elijah Muhammad rarely read the Qur'an or the Bible in any other way. Such a comparison must, of course, be used with caution. Applied too narrowly and without qualifications, it could lead one to suggest that Elijah Muhammad considered Fard Muhammad an incarnation of Allah. Druze and Alawites certainly may consider Ali and others as human beings embodying Allah, but for Elijah Muhammad, Fard Muhammad *was* Allah – not an embodiment or incarnation of Allah; "incarnation," particularly one similar to Christian teachings about Jesus, suggested a spiritualized conception of Allah – as a "mystery God" – that Elijah Muhammad adamantly rejected. The periodic presence of God among humans he accepted, but not the periodic incarnation of some spiritual deity. Being initially unaware of the Shari'a and, if he became aware later, being uninterested in it, is not the same as rejecting it. For Elijah Muhammad the defining characteristic of scripture was its hidden prophecies. He did not accept reincarnation, another common doctrine among the ghulat. Such claims in relation to Fard Muhammad appear only in outside sources, never within the Nation of Islam. Nevertheless, a comparison with the ghulat does highlight that Elijah Muhammad's teachings are not as unprecedented in Islam or as distant from other formulations of Islam as they are so frequently portrayed.

1

ISLAM AND AFRICAN AMERICANS

Islam came to the land that would become the United States of America as early as 1527, with the presence of Estevan or Stephen the Moor, a Moroccan Muslim (at least originally) who came to the Florida peninsula with a Spanish fleet. Like so many Africans who were brought to the Americas thereafter, he was a slave. The approximately two million African Americans who are Muslims today are not so because of Estevan, however, and not even because of the thousands of African Muslims later brought to the shores of North America and sold as slaves. Elijah Muhammad, who assumed that all Africans enslaved in the United States had been Muslims and that the only natural religion for their descendants was Islam, had to re-create that Muslim legacy *ex nihilo*.

AFRICAN AMERICAN MUSLIM SLAVES AND AFRICAN AMERICAN RELIGION

Approximately twelve million Africans were shipped from Africa to the Americas as slaves. Of those, about half a million were shipped to British colonies in North America and later to the United States. The transatlantic slave trade began when Spanish colonies imported Africans as slaves in the second half of the sixteenth century. Virginia, an English colony, began in 1619. By the mid-nineteenth century, their descendants, most of whom were still slaves, numbered some four million. Initially, slavery had not been completely racialized. There were a few white and Native American slaves and even a few black slave-owners. Although people of European descent continued to be indentured servants for quite some time, racialized chattel slavery – in which only African slaves and their offspring were owned by whites – soon became the norm.

Determining how many of these imported Africans were Muslims is difficult. Their religious affiliations were of little interest to either the slavers or the slave-owners. Moreover, slaves were systematically stripped of ties to their homeland, including names, family or tribal bonds, and culture. There is evidence that some of the newly imported slaves made efforts to preserve their African religious traditions, including Islam, especially within their own families. But such evidence is by nature limited, for they would have had to do so secretly. That some slaves were Muslim is obvious from names recorded in ledgers and runaway notices, the latter of which specified names and provided descriptions, including occasionally ethnicity or geographical origins. Estimates of the number of Muslim Africans brought to the colonies and the United States must largely be based on the presumed proportion of Muslims in the African regions from which they were originally purchased or captured. Over half of the Africans came from West Africa, a region where Islam was prevalent, and perhaps fifteen percent were Muslims.

Because Islam's introduction into West Africa promoted literacy, there were some noteworthy literate Muslim slaves. Their literacy brought them fame, freedom, and for some the opportunity to return to Africa. Job Ben Solomon (d. 1773) was born Hyuba boon Salumena boon Hibrahema (or Ayyub b. Sulayman

b. Ibrahim) in around 1702 in what is now Senegal. Sent by his father, an imam, to sell two slaves and to buy paper, he was himself enslaved and sent to Annapolis, Maryland. He continued to practice Islam, ran away, but he was caught and imprisoned. He was freed from prison and slavery when he was purchased by a man impressed with his religious devotion and his knowledge of Arabic. On a trip to England, Job wrote out the Qur'an in Arabic from memory. After gaining some fame in England, he secured his return to Africa in 1734, where he attempted to engage in trade on behalf of the British. Abd ar-Rahman Ibrahima (d. 1829) endured forty years of slavery, as opposed to Job's three. He was born in 1762, son of the King of Timbo in modern-day Guinea. In 1787 Ibrahima led troops into battle, was defeated, and captured. After surviving the Middle Passage, he was sold as a slave in Mississippi in 1788. He too attempted to run away, but was unsuccessful. He remained a slave, married and raised a family, and became an overseer for his owner. He only obtained manumission by writing a letter that made it to the King of Morocco in 1827. Afterward, he lectured in the northeast of the USA and earned enough money to free his children. He enlisted the aid of the American Colonization Society to get himself and his wife to Liberia, promising to preach Christianity and facilitate trade there. Whether this was a ruse is uncertain, for he died very shortly after arriving back in Africa in 1829. Lamine Kebe (d. after 1837) had a similar story. He was born around 1780 in Futa Jallon to a family of scholars and clerics. He had seven years of advanced Islamic education, including the study of the Qur'an and its exegesis, hadith studies, theology, law, and philology, and was himself a teacher. In his mid-twenties, he was captured and arrived in the United States in 1807, spending most of the next three decades as a slave in Georgia, South Carolina, and Alabama. He secured his return to Africa in 1835 by convincing white philanthropists that he would serve as a Christian missionary. Umar ibn Said

(d. 1864) is the best-known Muslim slave, for he wrote an autobiography and fourteen of his Arabic manuscripts remain extant. He too was born in or near modern-day Senegal, in 1770. He trained as a scholar, was captured during war and enslaved. He arrived in Charleston, South Carolina in 1807, the last year that Africans could be legally imported as slaves. His second master was such a hard taskmaster that he too ran away, only to be captured in a church in North Carolina where he was praying. His Arabic writing caught the attention of the brother of the state governor. In 1821 he converted to Christianity and was baptized, but his many Arabic manuscripts containing references to Muhammad suggest that his conversion was feigned. When asked to write the Christian "Lord's Prayer" in Arabic, he often simply paraphrased Qur'an 110.

These four men were truly remarkable men and remarkable Muslims. Most tried to escape enslavement and practiced Islam despite opposition – feigning Christianity only as long as necessary. To them could be added perhaps a hundred other Muslim slaves for whom we have some evidence of their attempts to preserve their religion in a new and hostile land. There may be thousands more who did the same, but for whom no records survive. Two further Muslim African slaves, Bilali Muhammad and Salih Bilali, merit attention because they and their families maintained their Islamic identity longer than anyone else, one on Sapelo Island and the other on St. Simon's Island, both in Georgia and both less than two hundred miles from the birthplace of Elijah Muhammad. The former was also born in Timbo and well educated, for he was buried with his Arabic manuscript containing selections from the Maliki legal treatise *al-Risala*. His master placed him in charge of approximately five hundred slaves and even issued him with muskets to lead eighty of his fellow slaves to defend the island against the British in the war of 1812. Nearby on another island lived Salih Bilali, born in Massina in 1765. He too became a trusted overseer. His family, like that of Bilali Muhammad, preserved an Islamic identity, including a Muslim diet and clothing. There is no evidence, however, to suggest that Elijah Muhammad had any contact with these Muslims.

But the aforementioned African American Muslim slaves were really the exceptions: for all others, Islam was wiped out. The languages, cultures, and religions of African slaves were stripped away within a generation or two. Slavery as practiced in the United States erased these many African ethnicities and identities, replacing them with a single racial identity, "the Negro." Therefore, Islam had to be reintroduced anew to African Americans. It may be possible that there remained an association between Africa and Islam with a few African Americans. But there was no Islamic movement in the United States to compare with the Caribbean and Brazilian expressions of other African religions such as Candomblé, Macumba, Umbanda, Santeria, and Voodoo.

This association or, more accurately, this perception of a connection between Islam and Africa may have made some more disposed to the messages first of Noble Drew Ali and his Moorish Science Temple and then of Wali Fard Muhammad and his Nation of Islam. Perhaps even more important for the later success of Islam, at least for some African Americans, was their bitterness toward white Christian racism. Not only was Christianity the predominant religion of the white slave-owners and, after slavery was abolished, of the white racists who tormented many African Americans, but the scriptures of Christianity had also been employed by some ministers to support slavery and racism. Christianity was also the religion of *white* Europeans and their *white* American descendants. These were certainly factors that both Drew Ali and Elijah Muhammad emphasized. When various forms of Islam were reintroduced to African Americans, they were often explicitly anti-Christian.

Sherman A. Jackson suggests an explanation for this form of Islam and for the fact that most African Americans became and remained Christian. The outcome of slavery and subsequent enduring racism for African Americans was a unique expression of American religiosity that Jackson terms "Black Religion." The key element in this Black Religion is its "holy protest" against white supremacy and anti-black racism. Black Religion could also be clothed in any religion. Most African Americans appropriated Christianity to voice this protest, while at the same time rejecting traditional Christian authorities. Some African Americans, however, led by Drew Ali, Fard Muhammad, and most importantly Elijah Muhammad, appropriated Islam for the same purpose, without deference to traditional sources of authority. Jackson argues: "A black adopts Islam or Christianity … not in order to become an honorary Arab or white but in order to become a truer, more authentic 'black man!'" (Jackson, 28)

Jackson's thesis is problematic in that Black Religion has no independent existence apart from religions such as Islam and Christianity. Arguably, Jackson has merely reified a few salient characteristics of particularly politically active expressions of these religions among African Americans. Nor does he indicate why such a protest against racism need be "holy" or religious in nature. If black protest against white racism in the United States appropriated religious language from Christianity and (in the case of Elijah Muhammad) Islam, it also appropriated political language from nationalism in the case of the Universal Negro Improvement Association (U.N.I.A.) – the movement founded by Marcus Garvey in 1914 to advocate global pan-Africanism and economic empowerment. Thus a category of black protest seems more appropriate than Black Religion. Be that as it may, Jackson more convincingly argues that Islam had several advantages over Christianity that facilitated its appropriation by Black Religion/protest. Not only was Islam associated with Africa and independent from white Europeans and their American descendants, but it also had a reputation for resistance to these Europeans, a claim to an independent non-European civilization, a simple theology at least compared with trinitarianism, a conservative social ethic, a retributive justice from the Qur'an, a lack of an ecclesiastical hierarchy in Sunni Islam, and, perhaps most importantly, white Americans hated and feared Islam (Jackson, 44). In the cultural rhetoric of white America, Islam had since the seventeenth century been idealized as the antithesis of an America imagined to be democratic, Christian, and virtuous (Marr).

AHMADIS AND THE MOORISH SCIENCE TEMPLE

Between 1875 and 1921 Muslim Arabs immigrated to the USA primarily from Syria, Lebanon, Jordan, and Palestine. These new arrivals displayed little missionary zeal. The first Muslim missionary was actually a white American, Muhammad Alexander Russell Webb (d. 1916), who had converted to Islam in the Philippines. He established the American Muslim Brotherhood in New York City upon his return to the United States in 1893. His message of universal brotherhood made few converts. Antecedents for prominent features of Elijah Muhammad's Islam, however, can be found in the teachings of two African American Christian clergy: the pan-Africanism of Edward Wilmot Blyden (d. 1912) and the proclamation that "God is a Negro" by Henry McNeal Turner (d. 1915).

The first Muslim-born missionary to come to the United States was an Ahmadi mufti, Muhammad Sadiq, who arrived in the United States in 1920, and who came to focus his proselytizing on African Americans. Although he criticized the racism of Christians, his message still emphasized racial harmony. He had limited success making converts, but his movement greatly influenced Elijah Muhammad because the 1917 Ahmadiyya translation of the Qur'an by Maulana Muhammad Ali would find its way to him. Meanwhile, Shaykh Daoud Ahmed Faisal, a Morocco-born Muslim, established the first Sunni African American organization in New York City in 1924. By then, however, the first indigenous African American formulation of Islam had already been established by Noble Drew Ali across the Hudson River in Newark, New Jersey.

Timothy Drew was born in 1886 in North Carolina, a descendant of former slaves who lived among Cherokee Indians. The details of his youth as they have been preserved are vague and hagiographic. He founded the Canaanite Temple in 1913 in Newark, which owed far more to Christianity and Freemasonry. He used the name "Moslem" for his followers, and in 1918 an Arab Muslim immigrant discovered Drew Ali's followers. His better-informed account of Muslim beliefs and practices sparked tensions within the movement and led to a split. The Newark group became the Moabite Temple of the World, while Drew Ali relocated to Chicago in 1919 and formed the Moorish Divine National Movement, and after at least one further name change, founded the Moorish Science Temple of America, Inc. in 1928. He claimed that it was founded in 1913 in Newark, so he must have seen it as a continuation of his Canaanite Temple.

Drew Ali claimed that years earlier he had passed a test in the Pyramid of Cheops and, as a result, became Sharif Abdul Ali or Noble Drew Ali. In 1927, his "prophethood" was evidenced by a book: *The Holy Koran of the Moorish Science Temple of America* – more commonly known as the *Circle Seven Koran*, because of the symbol on the cover. The symbol, like much of the contents of his *Circle Seven Koran*, was drawn from Levi H. Dowling's *The Aquarian Gospel of Jesus the Christ* published in 1908 (and most of the remainder was taken from Sri Ramatherio's 1925 edition of *Unto Thee I Grant*). Two years later, Drew Ali died under suspicious circumstances, after having been apparently falsely charged with murder. He was released on bond before the trial and died, some said from a police beating, while others said at the hands of rivals. His movement peaked with some thirty thousand members in the 1930s, then fractured, but survives until today. Contemporary Moorish Americans or "Moslems" (as they still identify themselves) continue to use Drew Ali's *Circle Seven Koran* as their scripture and to view Drew Ali as their prophet.

Drew Ali had at least passing familiarity with traditional Islam. He mentioned Muhammad and the origination of Islam in the Arabian Peninsula and the later contributions of Muslims to the world's culture. He wrote: "The Koran should be of interest to all readers. It is the Bible of the Mohammedans, ruling over the customs and actions of over 200 millions of people. It is a work of importance whether considered from a religious, philosophical, or literary viewpoint" (Drew Ali, *Moorish Literature*, 20). His actual level of familiarity with the contents of the Qur'an remains uncertain, though it appears to have been negligible. If not so, then he seems largely to have ignored it, for he had little need of it. Like the titles of Noble and Prophet that he explicitly claimed for himself, like the sashes and the fezzes, and like the Moorish historical claims, the Qur'an validated his authority. What had currency was only the name itself: "Koran" and what it implied. Prophets produced scriptures and he was a "Muslim" prophet, so he used the name "Koran" for his scripture. Muhammad (unlike Jesus who was the main character in the *Circle Seven Koran*) had no such currency, so Drew Ali's *Koran* made little mention of him.

This independence from more traditional sources of Islamic authority and mythology is particularly evident in Drew Ali's formulation of Islam. Terminology is what really mattered for him. African Americans were not "Negroes," "blacks," or even "colored"; they were Asiatics, and more specifically, they were Moors. He claimed that the Black Laws of Virginia of 1682 exempted Moors from slavery. African Americans should never have been slaves, but the Founding Fathers of the United States renamed them Negroes in order to enslave them. Had Moors only "honored their mother and father," and not abandoned their natural religion of Islam in favor of Christianity, the tragic centuries of slavery would never have occurred. In that sense, both whites and blacks are responsible. Therefore, the latter must re-embrace their true identity, the Moors, and their true religion, Islam.

By accepting but also reinterpreting the racist identification of Africans with Noah's son Ham, whose son Canaan had been cursed to be the slave of his brothers (Gen. 9:25), Drew Ali identified the ancestors of the Moors with Canaanites and also the Moabites. These two peoples, along with the Hittites and Amorites, populated Africa. More recent ancestors founded a Moorish empire said to have ruled Asia and Europe from their capital in West Africa. Their dominion even extended to North, Central, and South America. Drew Ali's racial amalgamations of the Moorish ancestors seem to have incorporated all but the white people of Europe. In the *Circle Seven Koran* he somewhat confusingly explained:

1. The fallen sons and daughters of the Asiatic Nation of North America need to learn to love instead of hate; and to know their higher self and lower self. This is the uniting of the Holy Koran of Mecca, for teaching and instructing all Moorish Americans, etc.
2. The key of civilization was and is in the hands of the Asiatic nations. The Moorish, who were ancient Moabites, and the founders of the Holy City of Mecca.

> 3. The Egyptians who were the Hamathites, and of a direct descendant of Mizraim, the Arabians, the seed of Hagar, Japanese and Chinese.
> 4. The Hindoos of India, the descendants of the ancient Canaanites, Hittites, and Moabites of the land of Canaan.
> 5. The Asiatic nations of North, South, and Central America: the Moorish Americans and Mexicans of North America, Brazilians, Argentinians and Chilians in South America.
> 6. Columbians, Nicaraguans, and the natives of San Salvador in Central America, etc. All of these are Moslems.
> 7. The Turks are the true descendants of Hagar, who are the chief protectors of the Islamic Creed of Mecca; beginning from Mohammed the First, the founding of the uniting of Islam, by the command of the great universal God – Allah. (Drew Ali, 56–57)

Jesus too was a Canaanite, and Dowling's white, blue-eyed Jesus became a black Jesus when redacted by Drew Ali. From Drew Ali's perspective, it was the Romans who first killed Jesus and then hid his true racial ancestry in order to make him the head of their religion. Muhammad is not central to this mythology, and is mentioned only twice in passing within the *Circle Seven Koran*. He is the "founder of the uniting of Islam" and the one who "fulfilled the works of Jesus of Nazareth."

Elijah Muhammad would adopt the concept of "Asiatic" in which, if one is not white, one is by definition black. This was a simple mirror image of white supremacist ideology, but Elijah Muhammad either appropriated it via Drew Ali, or internalized that perspective in the same manner as Drew Ali. Elijah Muhammad's fear of integration, his portrayal of Jesus as a black man, his insistence that African Americans were by nature Muslims, and his view that Islam was the chronologically prior and epistemologically superior religion all owe much to Drew Ali too. Marcus Garvey, a contemporary of Drew Ali and founder of the U.N.I.A., had advocated African American return to Africa as part of his black nationalism and pan-Africanism. Elijah Muhammad would also demand not the physical return to Africa, as Garvey had, but a far more practical return to Africa, a spiritual one, just as Drew Ali had. Elijah Muhammad could not, however, accommodate Drew Ali's tolerance of whites, in which Europeans had Christianity, Moors had Islam, and they would live in peace when each worshiped "under his own vine and fig tree."

Two decades after Drew Ali's death, Elijah Muhammad explicitly acknowledged the earlier achievements of Drew Ali and Garvey, and saw their missions as precursors to his own:

> I have always had a very high opinion of both the late Noble Drew Ali and Marcus Garvey and admired their courage in helping our people (the so-called Negroes) and appreciated their work. Both of these men were fine Muslims. The followers of Noble Drew Ali and Marcus Garvey should now follow me and co-operate with us and in our work because we are only trying to finish up what those before us started.
>
> (Muhammad, *The Supreme Wisdom: Volume Two*, 84)

The ideas of Garvey and Drew Ali may have had a more direct influence on the direction of Elijah Muhammad's thought. Dawn-Marie Gibson argues that Fard Muhammad most likely used the alias of George Farr whilst in Garvey's U.N.I.A. Later, he infiltrated the Moorish Science Temple just weeks before Drew Ali's death in 1929 (Gibson, 35–40). Elijah Muhammad in 1965 adamantly denied that Fard Muhammad had ever been a follower of Drew Ali (Muhammad, *The True History*, xvii).

WALI FARD MUHAMMAD

The man who brought Elijah Muhammad to Islam is shrouded in mystery. To Elijah Muhammad, Wali Fard Muhammad was Allah; to American law enforcement agencies, he was Wallace D. Ford, a petty criminal and religious fraud. Elijah Muhammad emphatically denied that Ford was in any way connected to Fard Muhammad, despite the claims made in the news media and corroborated by the F.B.I. When the charge was made publicly that the man he regarded as Allah was none other than this criminal, he offered one hundred thousand dollars to anyone who could prove the accusation. For him, the accusation was just another attempt by the white devils to undermine him and his movement.

Wallace D. Ford

Wallace Dodd Ford's origins are much disputed. In an interview with the California State Parole Authorities, he said he was born in Portland, Oregon in 1891 to parents who had come from Hawaii. The same F.B.I. file states that he was born in New Zealand to a British father and Polynesian mother. He has also been identified as Jamaican, Palestinian, Syrian, Indian, Turko-Persian, or Afghani. A Detroit police report states that he was thirty-three years old in 1933, and yet another source states he was fifty-six in 1930, which would make his birth year around 1874, though Elijah Muhammad gives Fard Muhammad's birth date as 26 February 1877. After he moved to Los Angeles, he worked in a restaurant and married a woman named Hazel Barton, with whom he had a son. In 1918 Ford was arrested by the police but released. He is recorded as using the name Wallie Ford at the time. If Ford was indeed Wali Fard Muhammad, it is not clear when the pronunciation of his name became "Farrad." In early 1926 he was arrested for possession and sale of alcohol (that is, "bootlegging," since it was the era of Prohibition) and later that year arrested again, convicted, and imprisoned in San Quentin for the possession of narcotics sold at his restaurant. Police and prison records identify Ford as Caucasian or white, married, and the father of a five-year-old.

On his release in 1929 he made his way to Chicago where some scholars suggest he came into contact with Ahmadiyya Muslims and the U.N.I.A. He also seems to have had some familiarity with the teachings of Joseph F. "Judge" Rutherford, a prominent leader within the Jehovah's Witnesses. If, as suggested above, he found his way into Drew Ali's Moorish Science Temple as well, he was not in it long before its leader died and he began his own movement in Detroit, Michigan in 1930.

Detroit's Allah

We are on much more solid ground for the history of this period. In addition to the F.B.I. and police records, and Elijah Muhammad's recollections, we have a study by a sociologist, Erdmann Doane Beynon, who in 1937 analyzed Fard Muhammad's followers, by then under the leadership of Elijah Muhammad. All the sources seem to agree that Fard Muhammad began his life in Detroit peddling and selling silks door-to-door. Another early sociological study of the Nation of Islam, by Hatim A. Sahib in the 1950s, suggests that Fard Muhammad's story of coming from the East was simply a ruse to arouse interest in his exotic Eastern or Asiatic silks. In any event, this trade permitted him to speak to African Americans about his message in the homes of his clients. Quickly these grew into meetings in which he outlined the teachings of Islam, including the evils of alcohol and pork; soon a hall was hired and more formal meetings were held four times per week, often attended by hundreds. Increasingly, his message began to include racial criticisms of the Bible and Christianity.

And, he was no longer merely from the East, but descended from Meccan royalty, sent to bring freedom, justice, and equality to his African American brothers, the lost, now found, Nation of Islam in the North American wilderness.

What remains unclear is how much of Elijah Muhammad's teachings can be definitively traced back to Fard Muhammad. Elijah Muhammad would claim that all of them came directly from the man he regarded as Allah. Because of Beynon's possible connections to the Detroit police, there are reasons not to trust fully his 1937 description. Nevertheless, it strongly suggests that many of the major themes and features of Elijah Muhammad's formulation of Islam come directly from Fard Muhammad:

> The black men in North America are not Negroes, but members of the lost tribe of Shebazz, stolen by traders from the Holy City of Mecca 379 years ago. The prophet came to America to find and to bring back to life his long lost brethren, from whom the Caucasians had taken away their language, their nation and their religion. Here in America they were living other than themselves. They must learn that they are the original people, noblest of the nations of the earth. The Caucasians are the colored people, since they have lost their original color. The original people must regain their religion, which is Islam, their language, which is Arabic, and their culture, which is astronomy and higher mathematics, especially calculus. They must live according to the law of Allah, avoiding all meat of "poisonous animals," hogs, ducks, geese, 'possums and catfish. They must give up completely the use of stimulants, especially liquor. They must clean themselves up – both their bodies and their houses. If in this way they obeyed Allah, he would take them back to the Paradise from which they had been stolen – the Holy City of Mecca.
>
> (Beynon, 901)

Fard Muhammad's own writings are limited to three pamphlets, and are surprisingly unhelpful in tracing the origins of Elijah

Muhammad's Islam. "Teaching for the Lost Found Nation of Islam in a Mathematical Way" is a seven-page pamphlet which, as the title suggests, consists of a set of thirty-four mostly mathematical problems, but which have a deeper symbolic meaning. The other two pamphlets are known as "Lesson 1" and "Lesson 2," which consist of a series of fourteen and forty questions and answers, respectively. Beynon's description is reconstructed in part on the basis of these pamphlets. Most of the major teachings of Elijah Muhammad appear in these two documents, at least in nascent form. This is hardly surprising, however; the questions given in these documents are said be those that Fard Muhammad asked Elijah Muhammad, his new minister; the answers are those given by Elijah Muhammad. The origin of these lessons is explicitly ascribed to Fard Muhammad and Elijah Muhammad: "This lesson #2 was given by our Prophet, W. D. Fard, which contains 40 questions answered by Elijah Mohammed, one for the lost found in the Wilderness of North America, February 20th. 1934" (F.B.I. file 105-63642).

In his three-and-a-half-year ministry, Fard Muhammad gathered five thousand to eight thousand followers, including those of a second group of followers in Chicago. Most of these followers were, like Elijah Muhammad, recent immigrants from the rural South. Towards the end of his ministry, Fard Muhammad was seen less frequently at meetings at the two temples and he had his growing group of ministers, which included Elijah Muhammad, to represent him. Trouble was brewing. The police became concerned that his followers were not sending their children to the public schools, opting instead for the University of Islam set up by Fard Muhammad. One of his followers was accused of having performed a human sacrifice. (Beynon claims that the leader had asserted that Muslims must sacrifice four "Caucasian devils" in order to return to Mecca.) Whether this gruesome charge reflected a simple homicide or was a false police charge is unclear. The F.B.I. entertained the possibility that the charges were "trumped up."

On 25 May 1933, the Detroit police arrested Fard Muhammad. The police report lists his ancestry as "Arabian" and his profession as "minister." (His and Wallace D. Ford's police documents list him as Caucasian.) The F.B.I. report on Fard Muhammad claimed that the official police report stated, "[Wallace] Dodd [Ford] admitted that his teachings were 'strictly a racket' and he was 'getting all the money out of it he could'" (F.B.I. file 100-43165). The police ordered him to leave Detroit, which he did after meeting with his followers one last time. When some in the gathering began to weep, he said, "Don't worry. I am with you; I will be back to you in the near future to lead you out of this hell" (Sahib, 71). Fard Muhammad departed for Chicago, where he was arrested again and visited by Elijah Muhammad one last time. In 1934 he disappeared. In the 1963 article that accused Fard Muhammad of being Wallace Ford, Ford's estranged wife, Hazel, claimed that he had returned to Los Angeles in 1934. Ford stayed for two weeks, visited his son, and then left by ship for New Zealand to visit relatives. Elijah Muhammad, on the other hand, stated in the early 1950s that he received his last letter from Fard Muhammad in March 1934 from Mexico.

The F.B.I. claimed that the fingerprints from the Los Angeles police and San Quentin penitentiary for Wallace D. Ford, and those from the Michigan state police for Fard Muhammad, were all identical. Elijah Muhammad believed that these police and prison records, and the fingerprints, had been doctored. He offered one hundred thousand dollars to anyone who could prove that Ford was Fard Muhammad. In any case, such a claim was unlikely to make an impact on Elijah Muhammad; his understanding of Fard Muhammad had developed along messianic lines:

> He (MR. FARD MUHAMMAD, God in Person) chose to suffer three and one-half years to show his love for his people, who have suffered over 300 years at the hands of a people who by nature are evil, wicked, and have no good in them.
>
> He was persecuted, sent to jail in 1932, and ordered out of Detroit, Mich., May 26, 1933. He came to Chicago in the same year, arrested almost immediately on his arrival and placed behind prison bars.
>
> He submitted himself with all humbleness to his persecutors. Each time he was arrested, he sent for me that I may see and learn the price of TRUTH for us, the so-called American Negroes (members of the Asiatic nation).
>
> He was well able to save himself from such suffering, but how else was the scripture to be fulfilled? We followed in His footsteps suffering the same (persecution). (Muhammad, "Mr. Muhammad Speaks," 23 July 1956, 2)

At least by the 1950s, but probably much earlier, Elijah Muhammad had thus come to see the mission of Fard Muhammad as a fulfillment of prophecy. Also by then, his mentor's persecution in the mid-1930s had come to serve as his personal model for the persecution and turmoil he had witnessed.

2

ELIJAH POOLE

RACISM IN THE SOUTH

Elijah Muhammad was born Elijah Poole in Georgia in 1897, thirty-two years after the end of the American Civil War. The Emancipation Proclamation of 1863 issued by President Abraham Lincoln came into force in Georgia only when Major General William T. Sherman's Union forces conquered the Confederate state in 1864, thereby freeing over 450,000 African American slaves. The Reconstruction Era, from the end of the war in 1865 to 1877, saw the Southern states that had seceded being reintegrated into the United States and at least officially ensured that the newly freed African Americans were provided with equal rights under the law, including the right to vote and hold political office. The Constitution of Georgia in 1868 assured African Americans citizenship and male suffrage, but that same year the Ku Klux Klan was organized in Georgia. In 1870 Georgia finally ratified the Fifteenth Amendment of the Constitution guaranteeing the right to vote regardless of "race, color, or previous condition of servitude," as the last of the seceding states to do so, so that it could be readmitted into Congress. In many places in the South, however, white-supremacist paramilitary groups terrorized African Americans to prevent them from exercising those rights. General Sherman's "Forty acres and a mule" – that is, his practice of giving former slaves in newly occupied areas arable land and a mule for plowing – was abolished by Lincoln's successor, President Andrew Johnson.

The Jim Crow laws enacted by states and local governments, while nominally based on the principle of "separate but equal," not only enforced racial segregation, but also entrenched the serious social, economic, political, and educational disadvantages facing African Americans. Schools, cemeteries, and public parks were segregated, some restaurants and hotels excluded African Americans, and intermarriage was prohibited. Even separate Bibles were used to swear in blacks and whites in courts of law. Serving on a jury was limited to "upright and intelligent persons," a phrase used to exclude African Americans. In 1871, a poll tax was reinstituted, and some county officials were appointed by the governor, instead of elected; and, in 1908, Georgia adopted a literacy test for voting, the last of the Southern states to do so. In other words, African Americans were systematically disenfranchised. Similarly, racial etiquette required all blacks, regardless of social standing, to defer to any whites. Some whites in Georgia used lynchings to enforce racial separation and to terrorize African Americans, with 458 recorded as taking place between 1882 and 1930. And should African Americans somehow acquire political power or exercise their civil rights, there was the possibility of insurrection, as occurred in Wilmington, North Carolina, in 1898 when white supremacists illegally overthrew the city's elected government, or of a race riot as occurred in Atlanta, Georgia, in 1906 when a white mob turned violent.

Elijah Muhammad was born near the small town of Sandersville, Georgia on 7 October 1897. His great-grandfather on his paternal grandmother's side was white. This grandmother, Peggy, married a man named Irwin who was owned by Jane Swint and who had inherited him from her father, Middleton Pool Jr. Irwin had been freed when General Sherman stopped in Sandersville in 1864. Elijah Muhammad's grandfather, Irwin, and his father,

William, were untrained Baptist preachers. William Poole married Marie Hall, whose mother was mulatto, her mother having been raped by her white owner (though she maintained contact with the white side of her family). His father, William Poole, worked in the mills and as a sharecropper, renting land from a nearby white farmer for a share of the crop. To supplement this meager income, his mother, Marie, worked as a domestic servant for nearby white families. Thus, Elijah Poole, the sixth child of thirteen born to William and Marie, grew up in extreme poverty and in an environment in which his identity was almost exclusively determined by his skin color.

Like many sharecroppers, the Poole family fell into debt in order to make ends meet. They moved to a small town near Cordele, Georgia in 1900, probably for economic reasons, but perhaps to escape a scandal associated with pastor William Poole's indiscretion. Once there, William Poole again served as a pastor and worked as a sharecropper. Elijah Poole, like all the children, had to help support the family. He and one of his sisters chopped firewood on the farm and carried it four miles to town to sell it for fifty cents. Elijah Poole only attended school when he was not needed in the fields, and he dropped out of school in the fourth or fifth grade in order to support his family full-time by working on his father's farm. Later, he worked as a field hand and in a sawmill.

As a young boy, Elijah Poole once walked through a forest that his father forbade him to enter. He quickly hid when he heard people approaching. From his hiding place in a thicket he observed four white men leading a black man with his wrists tied behind his back. He watched silently as the white men untied the wrists and threw the rope over the branch of a tree, looped the rope around the prostrate man's neck, and hoisted up the choking man. He had just witnessed his first lynching of a black man by whites. Later, on one of his trips into town to sell firewood, he witnessed yet another lynching: this time, an eighteen-year-old black man stood accused of insulting (or raping) a white woman. There had been no trial, he had been lynched; he had been shot and his body hung on display in the African American section of town. The young Elijah Poole could not understand how his fellow African Americans could allow something like that to happen in their own midst. And again, when he was twenty-three, he witnessed the body of a young black man who had been lynched being dragged behind a truck. There seems little doubt that these firsthand experiences of the extremes of white racism in Elijah's early life shaped his views on race, and made him particularly receptive to Fard Muhammad's racial formulation of Islam a quarter of a century later.

Elijah Muhammad's leadership abilities and religious disposition were also evident early in life. According to Malcolm X, his mother described young Elijah Poole as a small, frail boy, but one who would settle the disputes of his older brothers and sisters. He displayed a strong race consciousness as a child, having listened to his grandfather's descriptions of slavery and his grandmother's tales of being beaten as a slave until her legs swelled. He vowed to her, "My grandmother, when I get to be a man, if the Lord helps me I will try to get my people out of the grip of this white man because I believe that we will not be able to get along with peace under his government" (Sahib, 93). His mother had a vision at the age of seven that she would be the mother of a very great man; she came to believe that the vision foretold of her son. Elijah Poole was also said to have particularly enjoyed his father's fire-and-brimstone sermons, and from an early age he was given to studying the Bible intensely, trying to unlock its secrets. Soon he challenged what he saw as his father's theological errors. It was assumed that he would follow in his grandfather's and father's footsteps and become a Christian preacher. However, from an early age he also questioned Christian doctrine, and he only joined the church under pressure at the age of fourteen.

As an eighteen-year-old, Elijah Poole worked for a cruel white farmer. He labored from sunup to sundown for fifty cents per day, later reduced to eight dollars per month. His boss humiliated workers who displeased him by holding them at gunpoint while his wife whipped them. Elijah Poole left his employ and worked as a manual laborer and foreman at the Southern Railroad Company and the Cherokee Brick Company. In 1919 he married Clara Evans, a devout Christian. In 1921 his father moved to Detroit, Michigan. Two years later, at the age of twenty-five, Elijah Poole, with his wife Clara and their first two children, joined his father in the northern city.

RACISM IN THE NORTH

Between 1910 and 1940 the First Great Migration from the South saw nearly two million African Americans move northward to the Midwest, northeast, and west of the United States. About 150,000 left Georgia alone in the two years prior to Elijah Poole's departure. Obviously, many African American were fleeing from the racism and poverty of the South, the latter aggravated by a boll weevil plague that devastated the dominant crop – cotton. World War I had interrupted the European migration but increased the demand for manual labor in the northern cities' industrialized factories, which had hitherto discriminated against African American labor. Many African Americans had also been conscripted to fight in the war. Fortunately for Elijah Poole, the war ended just prior to his being called up.

The prospect of greater freedom and reduced poverty had drawn Elijah Poole northward, just as it had so many others. But racism, poverty, and violence were not exclusive to the

South. In his first year in Detroit, he witnessed an African American shot in the streets by white police officers. Again he felt that African Americans suffered quietly and received no justice: "Now, I left the South so as to get out of the territory where such things are going on all the time and now I find it here before me in the police department. The difference is that they do not hang them up to the trees but they kill them right here on the streets" (Sahib, 90). Like many African Americans who had moved north, he found that employment was often short term. He bounced from job to job, often working in low-paying factory jobs. He found work at the Detroit Copper Company, the American Nut Company, Briggs Body, and the Chevrolet Axle Company. Even that, however, came to an end with the Great Depression: African Americans were the first to be laid off. In 1929, he lost his job and was forced to go on relief. Depressed and in despair, he began to drink, and one day his wife had to get him after he had fallen down drunk. Even so, he felt the need to be a better man. He tried to accommodate his "religious" inclinations by joining the Masonic movement. His childhood interest in religion had not waned; he wanted to preach. He just could not reconcile himself with Christianity.

THE NATION OF ISLAM

A solution presented itself in 1931 when Elijah Poole was introduced to a new preacher in Detroit: Wali Fard Muhammad. He taught that the "so-called Negroes" were originally Asiatics – the original people of earth. To attain freedom and justice, they must abandon the religion of the white devil, Christianity, and return to Islam. This return was also urgent, for soon the present world would be consumed in an apocalyptic battle between

Christianity and Islam. He also taught the more recognizably Islamic practices of avoiding pork and alcohol.

According to one account, Elijah Poole was introduced to this new preacher via his father, who had heard about him from his friend Abdul Mohammed, a former follower of Noble Drew Ali. Another account suggests that Elijah's wife introduced him to the movement in the hopes of curbing his use of alcohol. In any case, Elijah Poole and his brother were instructed by Abdul Mohammed before they sought out Fard Muhammad himself. The latter drew such large crowds that several times Elijah Poole could not get inside the buildings where he spoke; often seven hundred to eight hundred attendees tried to crowd into the meetings held in halls designed for half that number. According to Elijah Muhammad's recollection years later, when he finally met Fard Muhammad, he said, "You are that one we read in the Bible that he would come in the last day under the name Jesus. You are that one?" (Sahib, 91). Fard Muhammad pondered the question, and then replied that he was the one who has been awaited for the last two thousand years.

Elijah Poole's conversion was immediate and complete. He began sharing what he had learned right away, and searched the Bible to support these teachings. By the fall of 1931, his wife Clara had become interested and went to a meeting while her husband stayed home with their children. Fard Muhammad asked the crowd about "the little man from Hamtramck" (the suburb of Detroit where the Pooles lived). When Clara identified herself, Fard Muhammad instructed her to tell her husband that he had permission to teach Islam. Soon Elijah was holding meetings in his house and would go into the closet to pray to Fard Muhammad. At one point in 1931 Fard Muhammad came to his home personally to teach him about Islam, after which he came almost daily for nine months and then more periodically thereafter for fifteen months.

In all of Elijah Muhammad's later discussions of this period, he claims that Fard Muhammad told him privately that he was Allah in person. Yet it remains unclear how much of Fard Muhammad's elevation to prophethood and later godhood was his own doing. Fard Muhammad used the title "Master"; it was Elijah Poole who first called him a prophet and convinced others to do so. In a 1934 publication, shortly after Fard Muhammad's disappearance, he was still identified as a prophet, and seen as the fulfillment of the prophecy of Deuteronomy 18:18: "will raise up for them a prophet like you from among their brothers; I will put my words in his mouth, and he will tell them everything I command him." Later, after Elijah Poole had begun to preach that Fard Muhammad was God or Allah in person, he claimed that this same biblical prophecy applied to himself, not to Fard Muhammad. Interestingly, he said that Fard Muhammad never identified himself as a prophet or as Allah, only as the one prophesied to come in the end times to save his people – though in one of his later writings he does say that Fard Muhammad used the name "Mahdi" and identified himself as God.

The use of the title of Mahdi and of Arab names led Josef van Ess in the 1970s to speculate about a connection between Fard Muhammad and the Druze. He felt that the doctrinal similarities between Fard Muhammad and Fatimid caliph al-Hakim were glaring. Both were God on Earth, both disappeared but promised to return, and both reinterpreted the afterlife (van Ess, 203–213). This suggestion is intriguing because the Druze (or Alawites and even some Ismailis) are among those accused of being ghulat, and their teachings exhibit ghuluw characteristics: deification of an imam, reincarnation, rejection of Shari'a, and symbolic interpretation of the Qur'an. As noted above, these have some parallels in the teachings of Elijah Muhammad. A Lebanese origin for Fard Muhammad, assuming he is also Wallace Dodd Ford, remains a possibility, though it seems implausible if his wife's claim that he came from New Zealand is taken seriously. Moreover, given that Fard Muhammad had given Elijah Muhammad a Qur'an translated by an Ahmadi, Maulana Muhammad Ali, the missionary activity of Ahmadi Mufti Muhammad Sadiq among African Americans in the 1920s, and the use of the title "Mahdi" by Mirza Ghulam Ahmad (d. 1908), the founder and eponym of the movement, that term's use by Fard Muhammad need not have a ghulat connection. The fact that Mahdi is often paired with "the Promised Messiah" in Nation of Islam literature, as it is in Ahmadi literature with regard to Mirza Ghulam Ahmad, further supports a connection. Determining exactly how "Mahdi" entered into the vocabulary of the early Nation of Islam would thus do much to shed light on the mysteries that still surround Fard Muhammad and the source of the teachings he transmitted to his followers, especially the young Elijah Poole.

Elijah Poole became Fard Muhammad's third minister, behind Abdul Mohammed and Othman Ali. Fard seems to have been displeased with his other two ministers and so mentored Elijah Poole personally, by visiting him at his home. Fard Muhammad also renamed his most ardent follower Elijah Karriem. During this period, Fard Muhammad seems to have allowed his student ministers to choose their own minister from among themselves. Elijah Karriem, as the least articulate and charismatic of them, was never selected. However, before Fard Muhammad's disappearance, he broke with this practice and publicly endorsed Elijah Karriem as "My Minister," thus making him the supreme minister of the Nation of Islam. Again, the historical details of this recollection are somewhat problematic, as the early newspaper *The Final Call*, published by the newly renamed Elijah Muhammad, merely identified him as "Minister of Islam in North America" in August 1934 (shortly after Fard Muhammad's disappearance).

The final interactions between Elijah Muhammad and Fard Muhammad are not entirely clear either. Fard Muhammad had begun to recede from the public spotlight as early as 1932, focusing on administration and allowing his ministers to do the preaching, and in May 1933, he was arrested and ordered to leave Detroit. After he departed for Chicago, Elijah Muhammad continued to hold meetings in Detroit, but in 1934 he too was forced to leave for Chicago. There he saw Fard Muhammad for one last time. Sometime before that last meeting, Elijah Muhammad was given two Qur'ans and a list of 104 books to read. He received his last letter from his leader in March 1934, purportedly from Mexico. Even the F.B.I. was uncertain about Fard Muhammad's whereabouts; he had simply disappeared. But for Elijah Muhammad he was still very much present, continuing to communicate with him via verbal inspiration. Decades later, Elijah Muhammad told journalists that he was still in communication with Fard Muhammad at least once every year. He heard a voice in his ears: "I do not have visions, but I do have voices, at times ... I know God. I was with Him about three and about four or five months. I know His Voice. And when He Speaks, I know it ... It is the Same Voice. It was Him that I have learned all that I am now teaching ... Whenever the time is necessary that He Speak to me" ("Muhammad Meets the Press!" 3–4).

3

THE APOSTLE OF ALLAH

A DECADE OF PERSECUTION, PREACHING, AND PRISON

With five thousand to eight thousand followers in Detroit and Chicago, Wali Fard Muhammad had created a sizable movement. With his mysterious disappearance, however, it was not long before a power struggle erupted between his various ministers in the Nation of Islam. Abdul Mohammed hoped to gain control of the organization by teaching against Fard Muhammad. Elijah Muhammad retained the original teachings but deified Fard Muhammad. Abdul Mohammed was not his only difficulty. Fard Muhammad had established a school called the University of Islam, where members of the Nation of Islam could have their children educated outside of the public school system. When the Michigan State Board of Education had the teachers of the University of Islam and the Secretary of the Temple arrested, Elijah Muhammad turned himself in to the Detroit police. The charges were dropped, and he was given six months probation. One of the conditions of his probation was that he return the children to public schools, which he refused to do, and so the police continued to harass him.

Things became more serious, according to Elijah Muhammad, when his rival threatened him by putting a contract on his life. Elijah Muhammad escaped to Chicago in September of 1935, just as Fard Muhammad had done not so long before. As early as 1931, he and Fard Muhammad had visited the city and established a second temple. Soon after Elijah Muhammad moved there, the minister he had left in charge of Detroit Temple No. 1 broke with his leadership to form his own group. In Chicago, Elijah Muhammad fared no better. Other leaders of the movement, including his own younger brother Kalot Muhammad, opposed him along with the assistant minister of Temple No. 2. He was again forced to flee. Elijah Muhammad came to see these troubles as a persecution by hypocrites (for a discussion of this term, see chapter 7):

> In the fall of 1934 most of the followers turned out to be hypocrites and they began to teach against the movement, and to join the enemies of the movement. The situation got so bad that in 1935 it was impossible to go among them because it seemed to me that over 75 per cent of them were hypocrites. And therefore I had to leave them to save my own life. Hypocrisy was arising even within my house; my younger brother, who was living in my house with another assistant minister, aligned against me because he wanted the teachings for himself. They joined my enemy here and in Detroit and they began to seek my life. So Allah warned me to leave again and showed me in a vision nine people; among them was my brother. Therefore I left to Madison, where they followed me; and Allah warned me again to leave Madison.
>
> (Sahib, 80)

Elijah Muhammad recounted that during the next few years the voice of Fard Muhammad repeatedly warned him in order to save his life. Of the thousands of followers of Fard Muhammad, only 13 in Chicago and 180 in Detroit gave their allegiance to his purportedly hand-selected supreme minister, Elijah Muhammad. This wholesale rejection of Elijah Muhammad's leadership certainly seems plausible if the other ministers really held him in such low regard. However, he also seems to have encountered opposition due to his even more recent elevation of Fard Muhammad to godhood, especially or perhaps because of the opposite approach of Abdul Mohammed. In mid-1934, Elijah Muhammad's short newspaper, *The Final Call to Islam*, still only referred to Fard Muhammad as "Prophet" and to himself as the "Minister of Islam in North America." What he considered so obvious – that Fard Muhammad was Allah and that he himself was his prophet – was far less obvious to Fard Muhammad's other followers and ministers.

Elijah Muhammad spent the next seven years proselytizing in the cities of the east coast with significant African American populations. First he traveled to Milwaukee Temple No. 3, and then to Washington, D.C., where it is said that in the Library of Congress he read the list of 104 books that Fard Muhammad had given him. Through his efforts he opened and personally led Washington Temple No. 4 in 1939. Despite using several aliases, including Muhammad Rassoull and Gulam Bogan, in 1941 the F.B.I. took an interest in his activities in the nation's capital, especially since he objected to the participation of African Americans in a "white war" and spoke of a mysterious massive airplane that had been built by the Japanese on Allah's behalf to destroy America.

In 1942 the F.B.I. arrested Elijah Muhammad, some of his followers, and his eldest son. Elijah Muhammad had but a fourth grade education and was already forty-four years old – just one year short of the upper limit for the draft. Nevertheless, he was convicted for failing to register for selective service. After a year in a city jail, he spent three and a half years in a federal penitentiary. His only contact with his followers was through his wife Clara. Although he was denied a Qur'an by prison officials, Clara wrote out passages by hand or typed them and delivered them to him. He was released in 1946.

This seven-year-long period of hardship, from 1939 to 1946, seems to have had a significant impact on Elijah Muhammad's career. His sense of mission was strengthened. He may have only had a few thousand followers in the four aforementioned temples when he was released from prison, but their faith in his authority was strong. Just as importantly, his rivals had all but disappeared. His Nation of Islam was *the* Nation of Islam. During his time in prison, he had also acquired an example for his nascent "do for self" economic program. Just as the prisoners had to work to feed themselves, so his followers were to pool their money to purchase a small farm in 1945. A restaurant, grocery store, and bakery would soon follow. The goal was self-sufficiency, particularly from the "white devil." Moreover, during his incarceration, he also saw that no political, social, or religious organizations were seeking to help or reform African American prisoners. He decided to give this group his attention. After all, many of them had suffered under white racism and were most in need of his empowering message. This decision ultimately led to the conversion of the movement's most charismatic spokesman and missionary, Malcolm X.

TWO DECADES OF SUCCESS

Elijah Muhammad's earliest followers were drawn almost exclusively from urban African Americans who, like himself, had migrated from the South and had lived on farms. They had all experienced racism and extreme economic hardship. When there was employment available for unskilled labor, they were the last hired, the first fired. They were largely Baptist Christians, but with little knowledge of the tradition or its scripture. Only a few had completed high school. Malcolm X was a second-generation follower, whose background was more urban, but otherwise he shared their experience of poverty and racism.

Malcolm X, born Malcolm Little in 1925 in Omaha, Nebraska, was at the center of the Nation of Islam when it burst into consciousness of white America in the late 1950s. The son of a Christian minister and a member of Garvey's U.N.I.A., he was harassed and probably killed by white supremacists. He and his seven siblings experienced extreme poverty and were separated when his mother became mentally ill. At the age of fifteen he moved between Boston and New York where his illegal activities included gambling, selling drugs, pimping, and burglary. While engaging in burglary, he was arrested and given a ten-year prison sentence – a harsh sentence for a first offence. He claimed that he received the long penalty because of his sexual involvement with a white woman. In prison, he initially continued to be bitter, earning the nickname "Satan" because of his sacrilegious speech. Several members of his family, meanwhile, had become members of the Nation of Islam and introduced Elijah Muhammad's teachings to him. The two began to correspond. When he was paroled in 1952, he immediately went to Detroit to meet Elijah Muhammad.

Elijah Muhammad instantly recognized the value of his intelligent, now eloquent, and extremely charismatic new convert. And Malcolm X rose rapidly in the organization. Soon he was an assistant minister at Temple No. 1, then the minister of Boston's Temple No. 11, then of Philadelphia's Temple No. 12, and finally of New York City's prominent Temple No. 7. He was also sent around the United States to hold rallies and establish new temples. From 1952 to 1963, by which time he had risen to the rank of national minister, the Nation of Islam went from having approximately ten temples to having more than fifty. He also established the Nation of Islam's own newspaper, *Muhammad Speaks*. His rapid success in the movement and his notoriety outside it caused his rivals to become jealous. In 1963, he and Elijah Muhammad came into serious conflict and went their separate ways.

During this period Elijah Muhammad built an impressive organization. Soon after his own release from prison, he had his Nation of Islam purchase buildings for its temples. White and black Christians, and (according to Elijah Muhammad) the F.B.I., often impelled the landlords of the buildings that his organization rented to demand that it vacate them. In 1950 the paid members of the movement were just forty-five, including the Apostle, secretaries, employees of the Shabazz restaurant, teachers in the University of Islam, a few ministers and missionary sisters, a captain of the brothers and a captain of the sisters, and workers on the farm (Sahib, 109). The farm, restaurant, store, school, and buildings for temples not only made his followers independent of whites, but also served to isolate them from the larger African American communities.

The political structure of the Nation of Islam at the temple level had Elijah Muhammad, as the Apostle, in absolute control. Ministers served under him and were expected to teach what he told them. Under the minister were two captains, the captain of the brothers and the captain of the sisters. Beneath them were second and first lieutenants and then privates. Eventually there was a supreme or national minister and a supreme captain, who commanded the Fruit of Islam, the Nation of Islam's security force. Economically, the movement survived on weekly donations and revenues generated by the restaurant, store, and farm. Donations were collected for specific purposes, with different monies directed toward the Apostle, his family, the local minister, the University of Islam, secretary, emergency fund, the farm, the general treasury, and so forth. In addition, fifty dollars was expected from each member on Saviour's Day, the birthday of Fard Muhammad. Almost every day of the week had some activity, in a pattern initiated by Fard Muhammad. Services were held on Sunday afternoons and Wednesday and Friday evenings. (The nature of the services will be discussed in chapter 4.) On

Monday evenings, the Brothers (that is, the Fruit of Islam) met for instruction and martial training; on Tuesday evenings, the Sisters met. The latter meetings were called the Girl's Training and General Civilization Class; the training they received was in domestic duties. The Nation of Islam held an annual rally and convention every year on 26 February, known as the Saviour's Day rally.

Starting in 1956, Elijah Muhammad published a weekly column called "Mr. Muhammad Speaks" in a series of African American newspapers: *The Pittsburgh Courier* from 1956 to the summer of 1959 and the *Los Angeles Herald-Dispatch* from 1959 to May 1960. Thereafter, he published his column and many articles in the Nation of Islam's own newspaper, *Muhammad Speaks*, which had been established by Malcolm X, as mentioned above. With active proselytizing from the increasing number of temples, the columns in prominent newspapers, the growing business enterprises, and the annual rallies, African Americans were well aware of Elijah Muhammad and the Nation of Islam.

Until 1959 the same was not true of the non-African American population. In that year, however, the Nation of Islam, and particularly its fiery minister Malcolm X, began appearing on the nation's televisions, in its newspapers, and soon on its university campuses. After an innocent African American bystander witnessed a crime, a white police officer hit him with his nightstick, seriously wounding him. He was not taken to the hospital, but to the police jail. Malcolm X gathered the Fruit of Islam from his temple and they lined up outside the police station. The press took note of the disciplined, well-dressed black men who were not intimidated by the police. Soon there was a television documentary, *The Hate that Hate Produced*, articles in major magazines such as *Time*, *U.S. News & World Report*, *Newsweek*, and *Life*, and an academic study of the group by C. Eric Lincoln, *The Black Muslims in America*. The popular media were not kind to the organization, and it was this that prompted Malcolm X to begin *Muhammad Speaks*. But the negative attention of the white media did not hurt the reputation of the Nation of Islam. Quite the contrary, many African Americans were drawn to the man who seemed so to perturb white America. As a result, Elijah Muhammad's speeches were now regularly broadcast over the radio airwaves.

It was a time of fame and infamy for Elijah Muhammad, for the Nation of Islam also came to the attention of other Muslims who decried his movement as un-Islamic (for which see chapter 5). Even so, by the end of 1959 Elijah Muhammad was wealthy enough to travel abroad. Leaving Malcolm X in charge of the Nation of Islam, he flew to predominantly Muslim countries including Turkey, Egypt, Sudan, Ethiopia, Pakistan, and Saudi Arabia where he performed the *'umra* (having not arrived at the time of the *hajj*). Both the opposition from American Muslims and his experience of other more traditional forms of Islam seemed to affect his perception of the religion. He began calling the temples mosques, and his youngest son Akbar began attending al-Azhar in Egypt.

In 1961 Elijah Muhammad became ill with bronchial asthma and was encouraged by doctors to move to a drier climate. The Nation of Islam purchased a home in Phoenix and he moved there to convalesce. All of his eight children were in key positions within the organization. His daughter Ethel Sharrieff was the Muslim sisters' supreme instructor and her husband, Raymond Sharrieff, the supreme captain of the Fruit of Islam, with Elijah Muhammad Jr. as his assistant supreme captain. Another daughter, Lottie, oversaw the two Universities of Islam, while his son Herbert became the publisher of *Muhammad Speaks*. His son Wallace was the minister of the Philadelphia Mosque. Two other sons worked in the Nation of Islam's dry-cleaning business. To Malcolm X, his national minister, he gave autonomy over his speaking engagements on the college circuit. Malcolm X also spent a great deal of time defending his religious mentor and the Nation of Islam from attacks on television, in newspapers, and on the radio. Elijah Muhammad had given him a stern warning: "Brother Malcolm, I want you to become well known ... Because if you are well known, it will make me better known. But, Brother Malcolm, there is something you need to know. You will grow hated when you become well known. Because usually people get jealous of public figures" (X and Haley, 265). Malcolm X came to see this warning as prophetic; he just did not realize that Elijah Muhammad himself would be one of those who coveted his fame.

As Elijah Muhammad convalesced, Malcolm X increasingly became the face of the Nation of Islam. He later learned that Elijah Muhammad envied him his eloquence in front of the college and university audiences. When he spoke at Harvard Law School, he realized how much Elijah Muhammad had made out of him – a petty criminal arrested in the streets of Boston not so long before. He continued to report to Elijah Muhammad in Phoenix and Chicago, but tensions between the two men began to emerge. Malcolm X pushed for the Nation of Islam to be more politically active, deploying the Fruit of Islam in areas of significant racial tensions such as Birmingham and Alabama, but Elijah Muhammad always urged non-engagement. He also seems to have been influenced by other powerful people who resented Malcolm X's increasing prominence. They even accused him of taking credit for his leader's message. By 1962, *Muhammad Speaks* devoted significantly less coverage to Malcolm X, and he was encouraged by others not to hold such large rallies. Publicly, at least, even in late 1963 Elijah Muhammad still strongly supported Malcolm X. He made him the national minister and embraced him at a rally saying, "This is my most faithful, hardworking minister" (X and Haley, 293–294).

Malcolm X's dozen years as Elijah Muhammad's most successful minister were about to end. In the summer of 1963 allegations emerged that Elijah Muhammad had fathered four children with two mistresses who worked as his secretaries. Adultery was an offense for which members were suspended from the Nation of Islam. Malcolm X had heard these rumors as early as 1955, but always dismissed them. This time he sought out the former secretaries to confirm the allegations. He also discovered from them that Elijah Muhammad was convinced that Malcolm X would turn against him one day and considered him dangerous. Before meeting with Elijah Muhammad, Malcolm X approached his son Wallace D. Muhammad, and they sought to mitigate the damage by finding biblical and qur'anic support; the stories of King David's and Moses' adulteries might serve, they thought, arguing that a man's accomplishments should outweigh a few indiscretions. When Malcolm X then met with Elijah Muhammad in Phoenix in April 1963, the latter found the comparison with David appealing. On his return to the east coast, Malcolm X discussed the matter and how it should be handled with his ministers.

Elijah Muhammad, however, came to believe that Malcolm X was merely spreading the rumor. When President Kennedy was assassinated on 22 November 1963, he ordered his followers to make no comment. Malcolm X did comment, saying that it was an example of America's "chickens coming home to roost." He was ordered to be silent for ninety days as punishment and duly accepted the reprimand. In January 1964 he was removed as the minister of Temple No. 7. Shortly afterwards, he was informed by friends that members of the Nation of Islam were plotting against his life. Malcolm X left the Nation of Islam in March 1964 and started his own movement. He rapidly moved to a more Sunni formulation of Islam, particularly after going on *hajj* during an extended visit to the Middle East and Africa. He was immediately vilified in *Muhammad Speaks*, and his subsequent criticism of the Nation of Islam greatly angered Elijah Muhammad and others in the movement. Malcolm X, by then using the name El-Hajj Malik El-Shabazz, was assassinated in February 1965 by several gunmen alleged to be part of the Nation of Islam. Elijah Muhammad seems to have had no involvement in the assassination, but it has been argued that he set the stage by attacking Malcolm X as the "chief hypocrite" and a "traitor." It was Elijah Muhammad's soon-to-be new protégé, Louis X (later Farrakhan), who had stated that Malcolm was worthy of death.

Elijah Muhammad remained bitter for years at what he perceived as Malcolm X's betrayal, and became ever more resentful as Malcolm X's fame continued to grow. However, Malcolm X was hardly Elijah Muhammad's sole source of difficulty during this tumultuous period from 1963 to 1965. Two of his sons, Akbar Muhammad and Wallace D. Muhammad, began to have misgivings about the movement and to espouse beliefs more in accord with a traditional understanding of the Qur'an and Sunni Islam. Akbar was declared a hypocrite in January 1965 for publicly breaking with his father's teachings after returning from al-Azhar. Wallace had also begun to question his father's formulation of Islam after studying the Qur'an during his imprisonment for draft-dodging. He too was expelled from the Nation of Islam, and his financial support was withdrawn. Despite revealing some of the organization's secrets (for example, adultery, corruption, and alcohol consumption) to the media, he was readmitted into the Nation of Islam after Malcolm X's assassination, when he publicly humbled himself before his father at a Saviour's Day rally. Elijah Muhammad and his Nation of Islam had survived all this turmoil, but not unscathed and, in his last decade, Elijah Muhammad would increasingly shun the public spotlight and act more swiftly to quash rebellion.

A DECADE OF DECLINE

The final decade of Elijah Muhammad's life was characterized by various setbacks for the Nation of Islam. He was forced to make financial connections with other Muslim leaders and court their favors. Membership had dropped in the immediate aftermath of the tribulations of the mid-1960s, but that later rebounded. And, Elijah Muhammad once again had to deal with his health. In addition to bronchial asthma and high blood pressure, he now had diabetes. In 1965 he was again forced to hand over day-to-day operations to his inner circle for three months while he recovered.

During this period, Elijah Muhammad also devoted significant attention to his latest celebrity convert, the boxer Cassius Clay, now known as Muhammad Ali. The boxer had converted to the Nation of Islam in 1964 and featured prominently and repeatedly in *Muhammad Speaks*, particularly in the aftermath of the Malcolm X debacle. In 1969, however, Muhammad Ali was chastised and Elijah Muhammad condemned sport, citing Qur'an 44:38: "And We did not create the heaven and the earth and what is in between them in sport." Only in 1974 was Muhammad Ali reinstated as a member of the Nation of Islam and once again prominent in *Muhammad Speaks*. Muhammad Ali could only rival Elijah Muhammad over publicity, but it was potential political rivals that the latter saw as far more dangerous. In 1970 John Ali, the national secretary and the man who oversaw the Nation of Islam's finances, was replaced. This period also witnessed the rise of Louis Farrakhan, who assumed many of the positions that had earlier been held by Malcolm X, becoming Elijah Muhammad's national representative.

Lower down in the organization, power struggles also erupted. In 1971 there was an attempt on the life of Raymond Sharrieff, still the supreme captain of the Fruit of Islam. What were claimed to be reprisal killings continued until 1973. By the 1970s there were also rival African American Muslim organizations, many of which had split from the Nation of Islam. The leader of the Malcolm X Foundation was murdered. On 18 January 1973, seven members of the family of Hamaas Abdul Khaalis were also murdered. He was a former follower of Elijah Muhammad who had left the movement well before Malcolm X had done so and who had become a harsh critic of his former leader. The seven were killed in his home, including four infants (one of whom was only nine days old). In 1974, there were more killings, this time at the Orthodox Muslim Mosque in Brooklyn. Elijah Muhammad was not implicated in these intra-Muslim feuds, and Louis Farrakhan dismissed even the allegations of a feud as a hoax instigated to tarnish the reputation of Elijah Muhammad. For his part, Elijah Muhammad seemed primarily concerned with internal disloyalty. He wrote that Temple No. 2 itself was beset with hypocrites and disbelievers and demanded that his true followers not even befriend them.

Financially, the Nation of Islam was doing well at least on the revenue side. The businesses, donations, and sales of *Muhammad Speaks* ensured a steady income. However, that income proved inadequate because of corruption and extravagant expenditures. Whereas earlier Elijah Muhammad had reached out to leaders of the predominantly Muslim countries in order to bolster his Islamic credentials, he now reached out to some for financial support. In the early 1970s the Nation of Islam had purchased a $4.4 million Greek Orthodox Church in Chicago to house Temple No. 2. The president of Libya, Muammar Qaddafi, provided a three million dollar three-year interest-free loan. It is not coincidental that at this time Elijah Muhammad altered the Nation of Islam's fast from December to Ramadan and *Muhammad Speaks* became outspokenly hostile to the State of Israel.

By 1972 it became clear to those close to Elijah Muhammad that they should start considering succession issues. His wife, Clara, died that year, and his own health was failing. He contributed significantly less to *Muhammad Speaks*, which relied almost exclusively on reprinting his columns from years past. At the 1973 Saviour's Day rally, he forgot the year of Fard Muhammad's birth, though his health seemed improved at the rally a year later. Regardless, he refused to designate a successor. He seems to have believed that any successor had to be chosen by Allah and that, in any case, the Nation of Islam could run itself. Others, however, began maneuvering to succeed him. The stakes were high. The Nation of Islam had seventy-six temples throughout the cities of the United States and many of them ran Universities of Islam. Membership rolls were kept secret, but there were as many as one hundred thousand members. Assets including supermarkets, fifteen thousand acres of farmland, bakeries, restaurants, a fish-importing business, and aircraft added up to an empire worth forty-five million dollars. The three strongest contenders were Louis Farrakhan, Raymond Sharrieff, and Wallace D. Muhammad (who had been readmitted, expelled again, but once more readmitted). Farrakhan was Elijah Muhammad's national representative and two of his children had recently married into the Muhammad family. Sharrieff, the supreme captain, was a son-in-law. The Muhammad family stood united that no outsider should succeed the ailing Elijah Muhammad. Most of them, therefore, supported Wallace D. Muhammad, and Elijah Muhammad put up no resistance to his growing prominence.

On 29 January 1975, Elijah Muhammad was checked into the hospital. While there, he suffered congestive heart failure and rumors spread quickly about his illness. *Muhammad Speaks*, however, remained silent, publishing the first reports of his illness only three days after his death on 25 February 1975. The next day, at the annual Saviour's Day rally, it was his son Wallace D. Muhammad who prevailed and was proclaimed the new supreme minister. Almost immediately he began the process of transforming his father's Nation of Islam into a far more Sunni-like Muslim movement.

4

BLACK ISLAM

To reconstruct even a single teaching of Elijah Muhammad, one has to scour innumerable speeches, years of columns in various newspapers, and his many books. If one does, one discovers that over time there are developments and shifts of emphasis in his understanding of virtually every feature of his formulation of Islam. However, the core of his teachings can be found in his *The Supreme Wisdom: The Solution to the So-called Negroes' Problem*; *The Supreme Wisdom: Volume Two*; and *Message to the Blackman in America*. Of these, *The Supreme Wisdom* is just a 56-page pamphlet that contains approximately 150 disjointed pericopes covering everything from Allah's "greatest" teaching, "Be Yourself!" to an explanation of why Africans have "kinky" hair. Nevertheless, this pamphlet is most useful for Elijah Muhammad's earliest teachings received from Fard Muhammad. It was published in 1957, but consists largely of material drawn from the "Mr. Muhammad Speaks" columns of 1956 in *The Pittsburgh Courier*. In the 1960s, Elijah Muhammad added about thirty pages of material to this original text and organized these materials into twenty-two chapters in his *The Supreme Wisdom: Volume Two*. He clearly felt that these two works should be credited to Fard Muhammad:

> You perhaps wonder why we call this little book "The Supreme Wisdom." It is because most every word of it is from the Lord of the worlds, "THE SUPREME BEING," especially where you read

> of the History of the Caucasian Race; the History of the Black Nation and Prophets; the Doom of America – how she will be destroyed; the Hereafter; the Future of the so-called Negroes – "Tribe of Shabazz;" what happened 66 trillion years ago, 50,000 years ago and 6,000 years ago. All of the answers are directly from the mouth of Allah (God) in the Person of Master W. F. Muhammad, to Whom all praise is due, the Great Mahdi or Messiah, as the Christians say, and He is also the Son of Man.
>
> (Muhammad, *The Supreme Wisdom: Volume Two*, 2)

His *Message to the Blackman in America* (1965) is his most important work – a 355-page summary of his religious, economic, and political teachings and programs. Unique material is to be found in weekly columns that he wrote from 1956 to the early 1970s, and his various rally speeches and radio addresses. He also compiled out of these other materials several other books with more specific themes, including: *How to Eat to Live* (1967), *How to Eat to Live, Book No. 2* (1973), *The Fall of America* (1973), and *Our Saviour Has Arrived* (1974). Several other books listing him as the author were posthumously compiled from his columns, speeches, and interviews.

All of these various writings make clear that Elijah Muhammad's religion was "Islam." He taught belief in Allah as God; the reality of the devil; the mission of prophets such as Moses, Jesus, and Muhammad; the centrality of the Qur'an; and the rewards and punishments of Judgment Day. His followers also prayed five times per day, fasted, and abstained from pork and alcohol. Yet many non-Nation of Islam Muslims argue that his Allah was not their Allah, and his Islam was not Islam.

For Muslims to suggest that there are is a continuous essence in Islam that unites or underlies all (true) Muslims from the time of Muhammad to the present is hardly surprising. This is a claim that most religious people make with regard to their religion. For a scholar to do so is to engage in the crude essentialization of Muslims, Arabs, and the "Orient" that Edward Said critiqued. Such scholars are also guilty of crypto-theology and bad scholarship. If one examines the myriad formulations of Islam, or the myriad Islams, which have existed in the last 1,400 years, not even the unity of God or the messengership of Muhammad that is found in the declaration of faith (that is, the *shahada*) can be said to have been understood consistently by all these people who have called themselves Muslims. One could, of course, opt for seeing some more internal, spiritual essence that unites all these peoples and societies, but then one's position is theological, not a scholarly one. One could also speak of a family of characteristics that make something "Islamic" – any person, practice, belief, society, and so forth that shares enough of these characteristics merits the labels Muslim, Islam, and/or Islamic. The danger here, of course, is that one selects characteristics that define a normative Islam. Muslims, like all members of religions, engage in creating such normative definitions, but it is not the role of scholars. "When one permits those whom one studies to define the terms in which they will be understood, suspends one's interest in the temporal and contingent, or fails to distinguish between 'truths', 'truth-claims', and 'regimes of truth', one has ceased to function as historian or scholar" (Lincoln, "Theses on Method," 227). Therefore, an examination of Elijah Muhammad's formulation of Islam based on his interpretation of the five pillars and five principles is not intended to pass judgment on whether they are "Islamic" or to endorse a particular normative understanding of Islam. Elijah Muhammad himself listed them as characteristics of his formulation of Islam:

> the principles of belief in Islam are: One God, his Prophets, His Scriptures, His Judgment, His Resurrection (of the mentally dead). The main principles of action in Islam: keeping up prayer, spending in the cause of truth, fasting especially during the month of Ramadan, pilgrimage to Mecca, speaking the truth regardless

> of to whom or what, being clean internally, loving your brother believers as yourself, doing good to all, killing no one whom Allah has ordered not to be killed, setting at liberty the captured believer, worshiping no god but Allah, and fearing no one but Allah. These are the teachings of the prophets.
>
> (Muhammad, *Message*, 82)

What makes his Islam and his approach to these five principles and five pillars so unique is the strongly racialist framework in which they are set.

THE RISE AND FALL OF THE WHITE RACE

The central mythology in Elijah Muhammad's formulation of Islam was not the life of Muhammad or any of the other Muslim prophets. His discussions of such things as Muhammad's first revelation, the *mi'raj*, his opponents' attempt to thwart him, the *hijra*, the battles of Badr and Uhud, the conquest of Mecca, and so forth barely appear. Rather, the mythology was about the selective breeding of the "devil white race" out of the original black humanity by the evil genius Mr. Yakub 6,600 years ago, that race's enslavement of Africans 400 years ago, and the impending apocalyptic destruction of these white devils by Allah. This mythology frames his understanding of Islam. Moses', Jesus', and even Muhammad's roles are largely confined to futile efforts to reform or confine the evils of the white race. Elijah Muhammad seems to have received his myth of the origins and destiny of the races from Fard Muhammad. Over the next four decades, Elijah Muhammad expanded upon this mythology, not by adding new elements, but by reading the Qur'an and the Bible in such a way as to find support for it and add new details. Exactly how he did so using the Qur'an will be explored in the next chapter.

According to Elijah Muhammad, the history of humanity does not begin with Adam and Eve in the Garden of Eden; they merely begin the most recent and most evil chapter in human history. The proto-Earth is sixty-six trillion years old. (Sixty-six is a symbolic number within the myth, for blacks had to endure sixty-six hundred years of white rule.) Earth in its current form resulted from Allah – not the same Allah as Fard Muhammad – blasting it in two using a powerful form of dynamite and resulted in the formation of the Earth and the Moon. Allah was prompted to this massive destruction by his failure to unite humanity. However, a remnant of humanity, the tribe of Shabazz, survived the blast and settled in what is now Mecca and the Nile Valley. It is from this original, black, Muslim humanity that all humans spring.

All went reasonably well until 6,600 years ago, when Mr. Yakub was born in Mecca. Although black, he was an evil genius who began converting its inhabitants to his cause. The Meccan population became concerned, and he and his 59,999 followers were exiled to the island of Patmos. Mr. Yakub swore revenge. He used the secrets of selective breeding that he had discovered in order to launch a eugenics program: over a period of six hundred years he bred an increasingly whiter and more evil race out of his originally black followers. He did so by killing off darker infants. In so doing, he produced brown humans, then red ones, then yellow ones, and finally a blond-haired, blue-eyed white race of devils. Then, six thousand years ago, this newly born race returned to Mecca and quickly sowed dissent among its black inhabitants. Therefore, they were exiled again; this time marched at gunpoint to Europe, where these hairy, naked, tree-climbing savages lived in caves.

Moses attempted to civilize these savages, but to little avail. Later Jesus and Muhammad tried to convert them, but were also frustrated. The former was even killed for his efforts. There was hardly any point to their efforts, for prophecy stated that this evil white race would rule the world for six thousand years. But this period of white domination would culminate with their destruction in America, where for four hundred years the white devils had enslaved some of the original black humanity. The end would come when Allah, in the person of Wali Fard Muhammad, came to find this lost Nation of Islam in the wilderness of America.

Although this myth might seem somewhat far removed from the more familiar accounts of the Islamic prophets, Islam remains central to it. Islam is the only true religion, the original and natural religion of the "Blackman." It is as eternal as black humanity itself, and spiritual, mental, physical, social, and economic freedom from the white devil is only possible by returning to that religion. Christianity, for Elijah Muhammad, "is one of the most perfect black-slave-making religions on our planet" (Muhammad, *Message*, 70). It makes blacks worship a false, white god (and so worship the very devils that have enslaved them). Blacks are taught to turn the other cheek in the face of oppression and wait until the next life for justice. Islam offers freedom, justice, and equality, under the leadership of the true god, Allah, in the person of Wali Fard Muhammad.

THE FIVE PRINCIPLES OF ISLAM

If returning to Islam was the solution that Elijah Muhammad offered to the racial problems faced by African Americans, then it should come as no surprise that the major beliefs in Islam are also understood racially.

Allah and Allahs

The most problematic of Elijah Muhammad's teachings is that of Allah, for it will strike most non-Nation of Islam Muslims as a clear instance of *shirk* – the act of associating something or someone with Allah and often described as the quintessential sin of non-Muslims. Yet it is not quite the same as *shirk*, for Elijah Muhammad would likely have argued that all he was doing was associating an Allah with an Allah. That is to say, he taught that instead of one god, there have been many Allahs. None of these Allahs has been somehow wholly different from his creation or a "spirit." Each Allah has been a black man, the most recent of whom is Wali Fard Muhammad. It is not, as van Ess suggested, like the Druze or Shi'i ghulat who held that Allah manifested himself in human form or took up a human abode (*hulul*). That would imply a spiritual essence to these Allahs, and Elijah Muhammad repeatedly dismissed such a conception of Allah(s) – albeit usually in reference to Christian understanding of incarnation – as "spooky mindedness."

When Elijah Muhammad spoke of Allah, almost invariably he meant Fard Muhammad. However, scattered here and there in his various books and columns there is mention of this more expansive conception of Allah. In one column Elijah Muhammad wrote that in the past there had been more than one god. Each god ruled for a limited period, and the one before Fard Muhammad had between twenty-five thousand and thirty-five thousand years to rule. These Allahs seem to have had no relation to one other, and there was no periodic *hulul* or incarnation that connected them. Yet, given their life spans, clearly these particular men were not ordinary humans. But all of these gods were black. It was only with Mr. Yakub, himself described at one point as a black god, that "colored gods" appeared – "colored" being understood as a deviation from the original and pure black. Thus it is clear that Elijah Muhammad does not see "God" as eternal, omnibenevolent, or even omniscient. One of the Allahs, after all, split the earth after he failed to unite humanity under one dialect. An even broader conception of Allah is evident in his

Lost-Found Lesson 2. There, in answer to the question of where and when the Bible and the Qur'an were produced, he suggests a collective Allah: "The Holy Koran or Bible is made by the original people, who is Allah, the supreme being, or (black man) of Asia … [he] makes history or Koran, to equal his home circumference, a year to every mile and thus every time his history lasts twenty-five thousand years, he re-news it for another twenty-five thousand years" (F.B.I. file 105-63642). Elsewhere, however, it is said that twenty-three scientists produce a scripture every twenty-five thousand years but then wait an additional ten thousand years before giving it to a prophet, as was the case with the Torah, Bible, and Qur'an.

With Fard Muhammad, however, Islam can be said to be monotheistic. He is the only god of this time. Elijah Muhammad repeatedly critiqued Christians for their belief in an immaterial God, a "spook" god who is somehow not human. When other Muslims challenged him, he dismissed them, saying: "They are spooky minded and believe that Allah (God) is some immaterial something … The ignorant belief of the Orthodox Muslims, that Allah (God) is Some Formless Something and yet He Has An Interest in our affairs, can be condemned in no limit of time. I would not give two cents for that kind of God, in which they believe" (Muhammad, "Black Man of U.S.A. and Africa," 20). Although human, Allah is extremely powerful according to Elijah Muhammad. He can be in two places at once, and he sees, hears, and knows secrets. And he has power over the forces of nature (Muhammad, *Theology of Time*, 121).

Fard Muhammad's specific purpose was to suffer persecution for three and a half years at the hands of white people in order to fulfill prophecy, demonstrate the price of the truth, and bring Islam to his "lost nation" of blacks in America. His father married a white woman so that his son would be able to move more freely among the whites who oppressed his people. It is clear that Fard

Muhammad did not appear African, and even Elijah Muhammad once said that he was not recognized as "being one of us." Elijah Muhammad taught that Fard Muhammad had been born to the tribe of Quraysh in Mecca in 1877. Fard Muhammad's father prepared him for his mission by gathering knowledge from around the world. For forty-two years, Fard Muhammad traveled and studied in order to prepare himself, learning to speak sixteen languages and to write ten. In 1930 he came to Detroit to begin his mission: to resurrect the Lost-Found Nation of Islam in America by returning the people to Islam and Allah's law. After teaching his followers what they needed to know and appointing his successor, he departed, but continued to guide his successor, Elijah Muhammad, for decades to come. Elijah Muhammad was less clear, even uncertain, if Fard Muhammad would return. After all, his followers in the Nation of Islam would be sufficient to gather his people before the Last Day, when America and the white race would be destroyed forever.

BLACK ANGELS AND WHITE DEVILS

Elijah Muhammad rarely wrote of angels, and when citing passages from the Bible or the Qur'an that mention angels he rarely even glossed them. Given his aversion to the spiritualization of Allah, it seems unlikely that he understood angels as spiritual beings. When he did discuss angels, they were symbolic. Once he equated the angel of Revelation 18:1–2 with the Mahdi, i.e., Fard Muhammad: "This angel can be no other than Master W.F. Muhammad, the Great Mahdi … The Great Mahdi is indeed the most wise and powerful being on earth (God in Person). It is He who with a strong voice announced the immediate doom of America" (Muhammad, *The Supreme Wisdom*, 48). Elsewhere, his followers are referred to as angels who carry out Allah's work prior to the Last Day. The seven angels who bring seven plagues in Revelation 15 are described as human "Scientists" who assist Allah on the Last Day (Muhammad, *Theology of Time*, 527–532).

Just as infrequent is any mention of jinn. Once he discussed Qur'an 72:5–6, "And we thought that men and jinn did not utter a lie against Allah; And persons from among men used to seek refuge with persons from among the jinn, so they increased them in evil doing": on that occasion he explained that these verses refer to black men who look to the white devils for refuge. Elsewhere, however, when discussing Qur'an 72:4–14, he identified the jinn as non-Nation of Islam Muslims because this section in Muhammad Ali's edition of the Qur'an contains the subheading "Foreign Believers." The jinn, therefore, were white devils, specifically "white Muslims" who decry his formulation of Islam.

In contrast, references to the devil and Satan were ubiquitous in Elijah Muhammad's writings. These terms referred to members of the white race, both collectively and individually, who were unleashed six thousand years ago by Mr. Yakub. Every reference to the devil and Satan in the Bible and to Iblīs and Shaytān in the Qur'an is read as a reference to the white race. "Black," it should be noted, included for Elijah Muhammad anyone who was not white: "the people of Islam are the black people, and their numbers are made up of the brown, yellow and red people, called races" (Muhammad, *Message*, 68).

Black prophets

Almost as problematic as Elijah Muhammad's understanding of the qur'anic "Allah" as Fard Muhammad, was his use of the titles "Apostle of Allah," "Messenger of Allah," and "Prophet." As noted earlier, initially he employed the term "prophet" for Fard

Muhammad, whereas he was merely the supreme or national minister. Shortly after Fard Muhammad's disappearance, he elevated Fard Muhammad to godhood and adopted the title of prophet for himself. For non-Nation of Islam Muslims who interpret the qur'anic expression "seal of the prophets" to mean that Muhammad was the last of the prophets, Elijah Muhammad's use of these titles was un-Islamic. From Elijah Muhammad's perspective, these titles were fully justified; he had received personal instruction from Allah and been commanded to preach, and he continued to receive inspiration from Allah. Like Muhammad before him, he distinguished between those teachings that Allah had revealed to him and those that were his own.

Elijah Muhammad recognized earlier prophets, stating that the true religion of Allah and his prophets Noah, Abraham, Moses, Job, David, Solomon, Jonah, and Jesus was Islam. Adam, it should be noted, is absent from this list. For Elijah Muhammad, the creation story in Genesis and the Qur'an is not an account of humanity's origin, but that of the white race. In Genesis 1:36, which speaks of creating "man in our image," the "our" refers to the black humanity out of which Mr. Yakub fashioned his white race. Similarly, when Qur'an 15:28 says of "Surely I am going to create a mortal of the essence of black mud fashioned in shape," that black mud is Mr. Yakub's 59,999 black followers. Consequently, Adam becomes a symbol for all that is evil from Elijah Muhammad's perspective. (The Adam story is rich with symbolism for him; the tree of life is the Nation of Islam and the tree of the knowledge of good and evil is Mr. Yakub, and the expulsion from the Garden is the European exile.) As for other Islamic prophets, only Moses, Jesus, and Muhammad play any significant role for him.

Moses (and not Noah or Abraham) is identified as the first teacher. For Elijah Muhammad, Moses was the prophet who, two thousand years after Mr. Yakub's race's exile to Europe, first tried to offer Islam to the white savages and "bring them into the light of civilization." Those who followed him left their caves and were taught to wear clothes, make fire, and to cook their food. Some whites gave him so much trouble that he was forced to kill them, by tricking them to approach a mountain were he had hidden some dynamite. It is not clear where the events of Moses' life took place, for he is said to have spoken Egyptian Arabic and interacted with the pharaoh. The Israelites are said to have loved the Egyptians, who were evil and so were attacked by fiery serpents. Nimrod was born as an opponent to Moses' teachings. Thus the teachings of Moses lasted not 2,000 years but only 1,700, for they were cut short by the 300 years of Nimrod's opposition. (It was Nimrod who was born on 25 December, not Jesus, who had been born during the first or second week of September, according to Elijah Muhammad.) The few whites who heeded Moses became the Jews.

The story of Jesus is even more original. Elijah Muhammad explains that Mary had been disguised by her father in his clothes and a beard made out of goat hair to protect her from the insults of the white devil. When her father had left to oversee the construction of a mosque, a severe dust storm arose. She called on Joseph, an old man whom she loved, to assist her with the animals. Three months later Mary's father noticed that she was pregnant and feared that he would have to kill her in accordance with Jewish law. Joseph, however, was told by an old prophetess not to disown the child for he was prophesied in the Qur'an to be the last prophet to the Jews. She then taught him how to protect the child from the Jews. As an unwed mother, Mary and Jesus were in danger among the Jews. Therefore, after the birth of Jesus, Mary fled on a camel to Egypt – for both Joseph and Mary were "aboriginal Egyptians." Among the "black people" of Egypt, he was safe. In his early teens, an old prophet befriended him and told him of the qur'anic prophecy. After completing his education with the old prophet, Jesus returned to the land of the Jews, having made no attempt to teach the Arabs and blacks in Egypt and Africa; he was never meant to be their prophet – a point that Elijah Muhammad emphasized to demonstrate that no African American should follow this Jesus. In Jerusalem, he taught the religion of Islam to Jews, but all but a few of them rejected him. Eventually, Jesus learned that this race could not be reformed and they would continue their devilish activities for another two thousand years. So he decided to sacrifice his life for Islam. After an altercation with a Jew in front of his store, he was arrested. Agreeing to let the arresting officer kill him for a reward, he was stabbed in the back with his arms stretched out against the wall. He died instantly, pinned in this cruciform position until the authorities came. He was embalmed and buried in Jerusalem where his body remains under Muslim guard.

The source of this myth and its fairly elaborate details is unknown, but it clearly was not drawn from the material on Jesus in the Qur'an. This narrative may be influenced by Qur'an 4:157, which states that Jesus was not crucified but only appeared as though he had been. Even though Elijah Muhammad also claims that Jesus only seemed to have been crucified, he did not cite this particularly apt verse, however. The point of the story is to undermine some of the key teachings of Christianity, to which so many of Elijah Muhammad's African American contemporaries adhered. As we will see below, the Jesus of the Christian gospels, on the other hand, is primarily understood by Elijah Muhammad as a symbolic prophecy of Fard Muhammad.

There is no such comparable sustained narrative for Muhammad (d. 632). Even so, he is not superfluous to Elijah Muhammad's formulation of Islam. Muhammad was an important figure for Elijah Muhammad, who casts him as an opponent of white evil, a model for himself, and he was the prophet of the last messenger, namely himself. Elijah Muhammad framed Muhammad within his racial mythology, identifying him as an Arab, which made him black. Since Jews and Christians were white, qur'anic passages directed against them were read by Elijah Muhammad as polemics against whites. After the limited success of Moses and the failure of Jesus, Muhammad opted for a different approach; he put them to the sword, which held the progress of their evil in check for a thousand years, until they discovered the Americas. Thus it was through Muhammad that Allah had made the third attack on the devils. (The first attack was the expulsion of Mr. Yakub and his followers from Mecca, and the second attack occurred when the newly created white race was exiled to Europe.) However, elsewhere, Elijah Muhammad presented a somewhat less violent relationship between Muhammad and whites. The "imams (or scientists) of Mecca" made it clear to Muhammad that he could not convert the white race to Islam.

Muhammad was told that he could not reform the devils and that the race had 1,400 more years to live; the only way to make righteous people (Muslims) out of them was to graft them back into the black nation. This grieved Muhammad so much that it caused him heart trouble until his death (age sixty-two). The old scientists used to laugh at Muhammad for thinking that he could convert them (the devils) to Islam. This hurt his heart (Muhammad, *Message*, 116)

For Elijah Muhammad, Muhammad also served a paradigm for his own mission. He too would make no effort to reform the white race, but rely on the sword. Muhammad served as a model in other ways too, as Elijah Muhammad's own comparisons make obvious. Both men had little schooling yet had been given knowledge of Allah and the Qur'an, both had to awaken an ignorant people to Islam, and both were opposed by hypocrites from within their own midst. Elijah Muhammad claimed that Allah always chooses a messenger from among a people whom he intends to warn or destroy. Muhammad was an Arab sent to

Arabs; he was an African American sent to African Americans. Little of this, however, was based on the sira (that is, the biography of Muhammad) or the Sunna (that is, the paradigmatic example of Muhammad). Instead Elijah Muhammad used solely the Qur'an to construct his understanding of Muhammad. But one of his exegetical techniques was to read both the Bible and Qur'an as hidden prophecies about contemporary issues. There was nothing unusual in a Muslim understanding qur'anic passages referring to Muhammad as applicable to them. His more innovative tactic was to read those passages as applying to him *instead* of Muhammad. Thus, qur'anic passages usually thought to describe Muhammad were seen by Elijah Muhammad as prophecies about the coming of him (in much the same way as those about Jesus were taken to be about Fard Muhammad). For example, Qur'an 32:3 speaks of a people to whom no warner has come. For Elijah Muhammad, the Arabs had had prophets, African Americans had not. He similarly interpreted the prayer of Abraham in Qur'an 2:127–129 as a reference to himself. In fact, Muhammad's role in history, therefore, is as a prophetic sign of Elijah Muhammad's mission:

> Muhammad was born in the Seventh Century after the death of Jesus, the last sign of that last one coming with Allah (God) in the judgement or end of the world of the devil's rule. Muhammad turned on the light (Islam) in the ancient house (Arab nation) that had burned low since the time of Ibrahim (Abraham) and cleaned it up for the reception of a much brighter light of the Mahdi (Allah in Person) and His people, which will come from the West out of the house of the infidels.
>
> That last Messenger is the One chosen by the Mahdi, Allah (God) in person, in the last days whom the Mahdi finds lost and enslaved by the infidels in the West, of whom Abraham made a sign with a small, unhewn black stone and set it in the Holy City of Mecca and veiled it over with a black veil and destroyed or

discarded until he whom the sign represents is returned (the last Messenger and his followers).

Jesus spoke of the future of that stone in these words, "The stone which the builders reject is become the head of the corner." (Mark 12:10) Muhammad found the stone out of place and had it put back into its proper place. This act of Muhammad shows that he was not the fulfiller of the sign which the stone represents, but rather a prototype of that which the stone represents. Moreover, Muhammad's replacing and repairing the stone was a sign of the work of the Mahdi, who would, in His day, raise and put into proper place that which the stone now serves as a sign of.

(Muhammad, "Mr. Muhammad Speaks," *The Pittsburgh Courier*, 3 August 1957, 10)

Elijah Muhammad saw signs within signs within signs. As we will see in chapter 7, some Muslims objected to this kind of redeployment of their mythology. He simply dismissed these "orthodox Muslims" (as he called them): "Though they do have the Holy Quran, many of them do not understand the meaning of it and some of them believe everything that is prophesied in the Bible and the Holy Quran about a last Messenger or Prophet being or referring to Muhammad of 1,400 years ago [instead of referring to me]" (Muhammad, *Message*, 187).

Glorious, poisonous, and future books

Elijah Muhammad had a great deal of reverence for the Qur'an. This he had inherited from Fard Muhammad. As early as 1938, an outside observer noted that the Qur'an was the most authoritative text within the movement and that Fard Muhammad had only used the Arabic text. Elijah Muhammad had no facility with Arabic. Fard Muhammad had given him an Arabic Qur'an but later had to give him an English one along with the list of 104 other books to read. Elijah Muhammad mostly used the translation by the Ahmadiyya Maulana Muhammad Ali (most likely the first edition of 1917), though he recommended the Abd Allah Yusuf Ali translation as well.

In one of his earliest publications, Elijah Muhammad argued that African Americans had a desperate need for the Qur'an:

> The book that the so-called American Negroes (The Tribe of Shabazz) should own and read, the book that the slavemasters have but have not represented it to their slaves, is a book that will heal their sin-sick souls that were made sick and sorrowful by the slavemasters. This book will open their blinded eyes and open their deaf ears. It will purify them. The name of this book, which makes a distinction between the God of righteous and the God of evil, is: Glorious Holy Quran Sharrieff. It is indeed the Book of Guidance, of Light and Truth, and of Wisdom and Judgement. But the average one should first be taught how to respect such a book, how to understand it, and how to teach it ... This book, the Holy Quran Sharrieff, is not from a prophet but direct from Allah to Muhammad (may peace and the blessings of Allah be upon him!) not by an angel but from the mouth of Allah (God) ... to get a real Holy Qur'an one should know the Arabic language in which it is written.
>
> (Muhammad, *The Supreme Wisdom*, 50–51)

While most of this rhetoric seems in accord with what other Muslims might have said, his denial that Muhammad received the Qur'an via an angel is unusual. It reflects both his rejection of "spookiness," or the non-physical in matters of religion, and the manner of his own revelations from Fard Muhammad. Obviously, the references to slavery and the Tribe of Shabazz make it clear that the Qur'an's purpose and message was subsumed under Elijah Muhammad's race myth. Noteworthy too is that Elijah Muhammad had to explain to his readers that the Qur'an was scripture.

When it came to the Bible, he made little distinction between the Hebrew Bible and the New Testament; he did acknowledge that Moses had brought the Torah, though he rarely used that term. The Bible, while scripture, in his view was not to be equated with the Qur'an, even though he cited the former at least twice as often as the latter. Numerous times he described the Bible as a graveyard for his people and a "poison book." The poison lay in its teaching African Americans to "love their enemies" and "turn the other cheek" – that is, slave teachings. Although clearly dangerous, the Bible also contained truth: "I don't mean to say that there is no truth in it. Certainly, plenty of truth, *if understood*" (Muhammad, *The Supreme Wisdom*, 13). "The Bible means good if you can rightly understand it. My interpretation of it is given to me from the Lord of the Worlds" (Muhammad, *Message*, 88). The truth in the Bible resided in its racial history and in its prophecies for and explanations of contemporary situations and events. Of particular significance were the creation stories in Genesis, which for Elijah Muhammad related the birth of the white race; the Gospels, which prophesied Fard Muhammad; and the Book of Revelation, of which Elijah Muhammad said that it was written by Mr. Yakub himself and that it prophesied the destruction of his white race. Of course, these prophecies and explanations could only be unlocked by Elijah Muhammad. This approach allowed him to employ the scripture with which the majority of his followers were most familiar, but in a way that made them dependent on him for its interpretation.

From time to time Elijah Muhammad also mentioned the existence of a scripture that was yet to come. In his *Supreme Wisdom* he wrote that both the Bible and the Qur'an must give way to a scripture that only Allah has seen. It is for the period after the Judgment, whereas the earlier two were for the present world in which evil and righteousness were still mixed. He also wrote that every twenty-five thousand years Allah writes a new scripture and that the Qur'an will expire in nine thousand years. This seems at odds with his teaching that the end times were at hand, and that Fard Muhammad had already written the book, though the world was not ready to see it. The future book's relation to the Qur'an is confusing, for he also said: "The Holy Qur'an will live forever. Why? Because it has Truth in it. I will not say it has some Truth in it. It has all Truth in it if you understand" (Muhammad, *The Theology of Time*, 379). But then the future book, which he claimed to have seen, also seems to be called "Qur'an":

> Then He told Me, "I will give you a Holy Qur'an when you learn how to read Arabic. I made it Myself." He showed Me that Holy Qur'an in Arabic on September last but I couldn't read it. I could only recognize one letter in it, so I expect Him within a year to come back with the same Book … The things in books that I have read will not do for us to build a New World out of. We have to have New Teachings.
>
> (Muhammad, *Theology of Time*, 379)

It is uncertain whether Elijah Muhammad simply misremembered this event four decades later, or if Fard Muhammad had claimed to have written the Qur'an. The latter seems very unlikely, given that the more fantastic claims about Fard Muhammad, especially that he was Allah, seem to originate not with him, but with Elijah Muhammad. The production of a new scripture seems far more in keeping with his less grandiose claims and the model presented by Drew Ali, whose Moorish Science Temple Fard Muhammad seems briefly to have joined. It seems more likely, therefore, that Elijah Muhammad is reconciling things that Fard Muhammad said with his notion that the latter is Allah and that Allah is the source of the Qur'an. Elijah Muhammad's son, Warith Deen Mohammed (i.e., Wallace Muhammad), came to believe that this future book was, in fact, the Qur'an in Arabic, a fact that Elijah Muhammad only discovered decades later (see chapter 5). Warith Deen Mohammed postulated that the idea of a future book was a ruse and part of a secret plan by Fard Muhammad. Be that as it may, such a discovery may help account for his father's shifting and contradictory statements about the future book.

The Last Day and the Fall of America

For Elijah Muhammad, the most important prophecies contained in the Bible and the Qur'an are those of the end times. They too form part of the racial mythology. According to Elijah Muhammad, they have been grossly misunderstood by Christians and Muslims alike, for the Last Day does not consist of the end of the world, a bodily resurrection, and one's appearance before Allah to be judged and then assigned to the Garden or the Fire. Humanity is already in the end times, Heaven and Hell describe the contemporary racial situation, and the resurrection describes a mental transformation. The purpose of Fard Muhammad's coming was to resurrect the "mentally dead so-called Negroes," permitting them to free themselves of the devil's rule and influence, that is Hell, and achieve freedom, justice, and equality, that is, Heaven. The de-spiritualization of the afterlife (which is not in fact an "after" life) parallels that of Allah by Elijah Muhammad.

These end times, then, are understood in the light of the racial conflict between blacks and whites in the United States. There will be a religious war pitting white Christianity against black Islam. Elijah Muhammad's efforts toward economic independence from white America and demands for territorial separation within the continental United States for blacks (for which see next chapter) were, for him, necessary preparations for these end times. Only independent and separated would blacks escape the coming destruction of America and Europe. In that sense, his economic and political programs were as much a part of Islam as prayer. Many qur'anic passages about the Last Day were interpreted to be prophecies about the imminent "Fall of America."

One of the more curious aspects of this destruction was the Mother Plane, a giant spaceship or "human-made planet." Back in 1932 Fard Muhammad had taught that it had been built in Mecca and given to the Japanese for use against the United States. After the end of World War II, Elijah Muhammad downplayed this Japanese connection. The Mother Plane, he explained, traveled some forty miles above the Earth and had the ability to make itself invisible or hide behind stars. It returned annually to the Earth's atmosphere only to refuel its hydrogen and oxygen. The scientists onboard even know our thoughts. It carries fifteen hundred bomber planes and bombs (the same bombs once used to create mountains on Earth) that would be dropped on white cities and explode one mile beneath them. The wheel in the vision of Ezekiel, the Book of Revelation, and the Qur'an were all used to support this story. Natural disasters were also weapons in Allah's arsenal, which he had employed before, as evidenced in the Qur'an.

Elijah Muhammad was unclear when the end was supposed to occur. The end of the white race was prophesied (by whom is not made clear) to end in 1914, but a sixty-year respite was granted so that Allah could save the lost Nation of Islam. (The use of the year 1914 may show the influence of Judge Rutherford of the Jehovah's Witnesses, who claimed that 1914 marked the inauguration of God's Kingdom on Earth with the invisible return of Jesus.) Elsewhere, Elijah Muhammad wrote that the end would occur four hundred years after the first slaves were brought to America in 1555 (that is, after three hundred years of slavery and one hundred years of so-called freedom), though he may simply have meant that this was the time for blacks to separate from whites. And in yet another statement he predicted that the end would come around 1965. He always felt that the end was near, but admitted that Allah could grant extensions.

With the Fall of America, black humanity would experience peace, justice, freedom, and equality: Hell would be at an end. Death would still exist, though humanity would live healthier and longer lives. The resurrection as spoken of in the Bible and the Qur'an was merely a psychological, social, economic, and political resurrection by African Americans. Elijah Muhammad had made it clear that the white race (and any blacks who had not chosen to separate themselves from them) would be destroyed. Not even their language would survive – which was another reason to abandon slave names or "names of the beast." Twenty years after their destruction, only the "holy language" would be spoken (Muhammad, *Theology of Time*, 499). Towards the end of his life, however, he admitted that some white people believed in Allah and were Muslim, so not all white people would be eliminated.

THE FIVE PILLARS OF ISLAM

It is a cliché to claim that orthodoxy is no more important than orthopraxis in Islam, but this was not so for Elijah Muhammad. He wrote considerably less about ritual, except perhaps prayer, than about doctrine. And when he did write about ritual, he was far more willing to defer to other Muslims than when he wrote about beliefs. But he understood even the rituals of Islam, the pillars of Islam, within the context of his racial mythology.

Shahada

Lā ilāha illa Allāh, Muhammad rasūl Allāh is a confession of faith that Muslims employ. Elijah Muhammad and his followers were no different. The words "There is no God but Allah, Muhammad is his Apostle" were written on a banner above the stage at the

1964 Saviour's Day rally. But Elijah Muhammad had taught Malcolm X to close his meetings by reciting the Fatiha in English and to say, "I bear witness that there is no God but Thee and The Honorable Elijah Muhammad is Thy Servant and Apostle" (X and Haley, 214). Thus, though the *shahada* was clearly used, the meaning was unique: Fard Muhammad was Allah and Elijah Muhammad was the messenger. Furthermore, this meaning ensured that, when his followers read the Qur'an for themselves, they would read the ubiquitous phrases such as "obey Allah and his Messenger" as references to Fard Muhammad and Elijah Muhammad.

The *shahada* did appear once in *The Supreme Wisdom*, written in Arabic with a standard English translation beneath. However, it was sandwiched within a passage entitled "Description of Prayer":

> The Muslim begins his prayer by declaring that ALLAH IS THE GREATEST and that he bears witness that there is "No God but ALLAH," and that none deserves to be served (worshipped) but Him. He further declares that Muhammad is his Last Apostle (an Apostle whom Allah would raise from the lost and found people of the seed of Abraham in the Days of Judgement).
>
> (Muhammad, *The Supreme Wisdom*, 45–46).

In other words, Elijah Muhammad is claiming that he is the Muhammad referred to in the *shahada*.

Salat

Elijah Muhammad emphasized the importance of prayer above all other rituals. It was to prayer that he had turned, alone in his closet, when he first felt moved by Fard Muhammad's message. In *The Supreme Wisdom* he did little more than extol the virtues of prayer and quote the "Muslim's oft-repeated prayer," that is, the Sūrat al-Fatiha. In *The Supreme Wisdom: Volume Two* he continued to encourage prayer by simply citing more qur'anic passages such as 20:30, 17:78, 17:116, and 29:45. However, in his *Message to the Blackman in America* he devoted a major section of eleven chapters to prayer. For the chapter entitled "The Significance of Prayer" he used Qur'an 33:41–43 as its epigraph: "O you who believe, remember Allah, remembering Him frequently and glorifying Him morning and evening. He it is Who sends His blessings on you, and so do His angels, that He may bring you forth out of utter darkness into the light and He is merciful to the believers (Prayer is better than sleep)." He elucidated the passage by stating, "This alone is salvation, just to be brought out of the darkness of ignorance into the light of truth. Who is in more need of the truth than the American so-called Negroes who do not have the knowledge of self . . . ?" (Muhammad, *Message*, 135–137). In a description of the morning prayer, Elijah Muhammad explained that part of the prayer is known as "Fard." The significance of that, he elaborated, was as follows: "And Allah's using Fard as His name here on His coming teaches us that if we expect to be successful, we must bow in submission to the will of Master Fard Muhammad; the All Wise God in Person who is worthy to be praised and praised much" (Muhammad, *Message*, 146–147).

In contrast to this racial understanding of the purpose of prayer, Elijah Muhammad's discussion of the details of performing prayer is far more in line with mainstream Islam. But this seems largely due to his dependence not on Fard Muhammad, but other Muslims. For example, in a 1957 column in *The Pittsburgh Courier*, and again in 1965 in *Muhammad Speaks*, Elijah Muhammad directly quoted the preface of Maulana Muhammad Ali's translation of the Qur'an when describing the five daily prayers. He even quoted the notes appended by Ali. Elsewhere, when he suggested some prayers, he cited verbatim from an orthodox manual of prayer. For example, he included the following translation of the *du'ū' al-qunūt*:

> O Allah, we beseech Thy help and ask Thy protection. We believe in Thee and trust in Thee. We worship Thee in the best manner and we thank Thee. We are not ungrateful to Thee and we cast off and forsake him who disobeys Thee. O Allah, Thee do we serve and to Thee do we pray and make obeisance. To Thee do we flee and we are quick. We hope for Thy mercy and we fear Thy chastisement, for surely Thy chastisement overtakes the unbelievers.
>
> (Muhammad, *Message*, 155)

This exact translation was readily available in many prayer manuals. His dependence on such a manual is also evidenced by the chapter entitled, "Time of Prayer and its Meaning," in which he reproduced a passage adding no comments, interlinear or otherwise. In this case, the qur'anic verses were allowed to speak entirely for themselves, which was not his wont. Moreover, the qur'anic citations in the passage appear to employ a hybrid of Rodwell's and Pickthall's translations of the Qur'an, not Muhammad Ali's. It is also one of the very few times that he cites hadiths (that is, reports of Muhammad the Prophet's words and deeds on which the Sunna is based). Clearly his discussions on prayer were atypical of his other writings and dependent on outside sources of a more orthodox nature. For example, the subjects of ablution and modesty are consistent with Elijah Muhammad's teachings elsewhere, but their presence within a discussion of prayer was unusual. Perhaps Elijah Muhammad was far more willing to defer to other Muslims on this ritual because for him it was not directly related to his main concern about race.

Services were not modeled on Friday prayers, however. Newcomers were questioned and searched for weapons and other prohibited items such as drugs and even candy. Whites were not allowed to attend. Initially, singing was not permitted at the temple, because Elijah Muhammad considered it profane.

Later, after requests, he permitted them this hymn composed by an elderly follower:

> We are fighting for Islam / And we will surely win
> With our Savior Allah / The Universal King
> We are united with our nation / And is called by its name
> So let us fight ye moslems / Fight for your own
> Let us fight for our nation / And we will all be free
> Fight ye moslems / Fight for your own
> The earth belongs to the righteous / Fight for your own
> Allah gave to you and for a Nation / The sun, moon and star
> The best of his creation / He is giving to you
> So let us rise ye moslems / Fight for your own
> Freedom, justice and equality / We now must have
> Four hundred years enslaved for the devils / Lost from your own
> So let us rise ye moslems / Fight for your own
>
> (Sahib, 178)

Then the Surat al-Fatiha was recited, after which the minister began to preach, usually on a topic contrasting the superiority of the original black race with the inferiority of the white race. If Elijah Muhammad was present (having entered under escort by the Fruit of Islam), he would walk to the speaker's stand after the minister had finished while the audience cheered. He would then speak for as long as six hours.

Sawm

Elijah Muhammad advocated fasting, not during the month of Ramadan in commemoration of the initial revelation of the Qur'an to Muhammad, but in December to focus his followers' minds on Fard Muhammad instead of on Christmas. As we shall see in chapter 6, he thought the Ramadan fast to be misguided. In the 1970s, however, he began to encourage his followers to fast during the month of Ramadan. Members of the Nation of Islam were also encouraged to fast for at least three days each month. Their fasts were twenty-four hours long, starting at five o'clock in the morning.

Zakat

Elijah Muhammad never used the word *zakat* or alms, but the Nation of Islam collected donations. In the early 1950s, the major donations were paid weekly and included funds earmarked for the University of Islam, the Apostle, the minister, the restaurant, the Apostle's family, the secretary, the farm, the emergency fund, and the general treasury. The amount to be contributed was left unspecified, except for the donations to the University of Islam and the general treasury, which were each to receive one dollar per week. Initially, those who contributed had their names announced, but later those who did not make contributions were announced. Moreover, every Saviour's Day, every member was expected to donate fifty dollars, which were presented to Elijah Muhammad. Temples were encouraged to compete with each other for the amount of money raised or presents offered.

As needs arose, other donations were requested. When Elijah Muhammad purchased the new building for Temple No. 2 in the 1970s, all members of the Nation of Islam were asked for contributions. Other such funds included the Elijah Muhammad Hospital Fund. Solicitations for such special donations occurred in the temple and in *Muhammad Speaks*. General appeals were also published. For example, "Money Necessary: We Need Money for the job of self-help. We, the Muslims, have been able to make ourselves confident in the eyes of the world, and we hope to gain enough help to make ourselves self-helpers. Black Brothers and Black Sisters, do all that you can to help me to put you on top of civilization. Thank you. Allah be with you. I am

... Your Brother, Elijah Muhammad, Messenger of Allah, to you all" (Muhammad, "Money Necessary," 6). In addition, members could donate labor to their local temple.

Elijah Muhammad was very successful in his fundraising efforts. Others too saw that it was lucrative. In the 1970s Elijah Muhammad had to warn people in *Muhammad Speaks* only to pay their money at the temples and to the official secretaries. In other short messages, he requested that donations be sent directly to him and that members of the Nation of Islam not collect money on the street or at people's homes. The unscrupulous were going door-to-door posing as members of the Nation of Islam and requesting donations for hospitals and for other causes. The Nation of Islam also sought to stop the selling of "holy names" (i.e., X's that removed original surnames referred to as "slave names") and pictures of Fard Muhammad. Such things were free.

Hajj

Elijah Muhammad performed the *'umra* (the "lesser pilgrimage," which can be performed at any time but is normally performed with the *hajj*) at the end of 1959. He had arrived too late for the official *hajj*. Just prior to this trip, a non-Nation of Islam Muslim critic of Elijah Muhammad proclaimed that he would be forbidden from entering Mecca because he was not a "true Muslim." With his *'umra* Elijah Muhammad had cleared himself of the charge; other Muslims recognized him as Muslim. That his pilgrimage was about legitimacy and not religious duty seems clear from his very limited descriptions of the experience. He wrote only of the lightness and healthiness of the water from the Well of Zamzam. Not even its connection to the traditional stories of Hagar and Ishmael or its rediscovery by Muhammad's grandfather were mentioned.

Elijah Muhammad never encouraged his followers to perform the *hajj*, but he did send Malcolm X earlier in the summer of 1959 to arrange the tour that he himself would make. While the latter would not make the official *hajj* until 1964, after he had left the Nation of Islam, his 1959 reports were among the very few reports of Islam's holy land to be received by the Nation of Islam. Malcolm X noted that the people of Arabia ranged from "regal black to rich brown, but none are white." They were their "brothers of color" with "no color prejudice" (X, "Arabs Send Warm Greetings," 1). Because Malcolm X became ill, he could not travel to Mecca. Even so, Elijah Muhammad's concern was almost exclusively racial and not religious (insofar as one can separate the two in his formulation of Islam). In his own writings, Elijah Muhammad did not speak of the city as the site of the Ka'ba or even as the location of the *hajj*. It was primarily the direction of prayer that he spoke about because it is "the only holy spot on our planet – the Holy City of Mecca" (Muhammad, *The Supreme Wisdom*, 45). Its significance was not even as the birthplace of Muhammad, but as that of Allah, Fard Muhammad, and as the ancient capital of the Tribe of Shabazz. Pilgrimage to Mecca is mentioned but once, and only in passing, in his magnum opus, *Message to the Blackman in America*.

DIETARY RESTRICTIONS

Elijah Muhammad also never used the word *halāl*; his prohibitions on eating pork and drinking alcohol were consistent with the practice of other Muslims, but were taken from Fard Muhammad. In the mid-1960s he became increasingly concerned with dietary issues and published numerous articles in *Muhammad Speaks*. Later, he produced two booklets on the subject: *How to Eat to Live* (1967) and *How to Eat to Live, Book No. 2* (1973). His stated purpose in writing these columns and books was to teach his followers how to attain good health and to prolong their lives by controlling the food and drink they consumed.

The most prominent feature of Elijah Muhammad's dietary regulations was his prohibition of the consumption of pork. This prohibition, along with the requirement that his Muslims eat only one meal per day, were treated at length and mentioned continuously throughout *How to Eat to Live*. His arguments against pork did not rely much on biblical and qur'anic authority. For example, he argued:

> Beyond a shadow of a doubt the swine is the filthiest and foulest animal human beings have resorted to for food ... Worms and insects take to its flesh while in the farmer's curing stage faster than to any other animal's flesh. And in a few days, it is full of worms ... It is divinely pro[h]ibited flesh, and God (Allah) has prohibited you and me, my brothers and sisters of the Black Nation, from eating it or even touching its dead carcass. Please, for our health's sake, stop eating it; for our beauty's sake, stop eating it; for our obedience to God and His laws against this flesh, stop eating it; for a longer life, stop eating it and for the sake of modesty, stop eating it.
>
> (Muhammad, *How to Eat to Live*, 17)

Qur'an 2:173, 5:3, 6:145, and 16:115, all of which forbid pork, are not cited. Instead, he employs the prohibition against pork in Leviticus 11:7–8, the warning to those who do eat it in Isaiah 66:17, and even Jesus' casting of demons into swine for scriptural support. As in the passage above, Elijah Muhammad also simply claims "Allah taught me," and "Allah has said," with "Allah," of course, understood as Fard Muhammad.

This source of knowledge about proper diet was even more critical when Elijah Muhammad turned to animals and other foods not mentioned in the Bible or the Qur'an. He described chickens as dirty animals, though they were permissible; beef, lamb, and camel were also permissible, but should be avoided if possible; rabbit, deer, raccoons, possums, turtles, turtle eggs, and frog legs were forbidden. That commands of Fard Muhammad and those of the Qur'an were blurred together was also evident: "The main thing Allah, as well as the Qur-an, reminds us of is that when it comes to meat and fish, Allah forbids us to eat the flesh of swine or of fish weighing 50 pounds or more" (Muhammad, *How to Eat to Live*, 60). It seems clear that he received some opposition, possibly to his restrictions, but more likely to the justifications that he used: "The hog is a grafted animal, so says Allah to me – grafted from rat, cat and dog. Don't question me. This is what Allah has said, believe it or leave it alone" (Muhammad, *How to Eat to Live*, 70).

Other dietary regulations promulgated by Elijah Muhammad needed no explicit divine source. He also prohibited collard greens, turnip leaves, white potatoes, sweet potatoes, peas, beans (except for the small navy, brown, and pink beans, and white beans), and corn bread. Spinach, rutabaga, and rice were acceptable, but to be consumed in moderation. There were no restrictions on garlic, onions, fruits (though they were better raw than cooked), wholewheat bread (as long as it was not fresh), and young pigeons. He claimed that these restricted foods had been cheap foods given to slaves by their slave-masters, unfit for human consumption, suitable only for hogs, or not digestible for those with office jobs. That Genesis relates that Adam was permitted to eat whatever he wanted, simply indicated for him that the white race ate much that was poisonous. Thus, even his dietary regulations are related to his racial concerns.

5

WHAT MUSLIMS BELIEVE AND WHAT MUSLIMS WANT

Given the fairly well-developed doctrines and practices described in the previous chapter, one might be surprised by much of the content of this "Muslim declaration" that was repeatedly published in *Muhammad Speaks*:

What Muslims Believe

1. WE BELIEVE in the One God Whose proper Name is Allah.
2. WE BELIEVE in the Holy Qur'an and in the Scriptures of all the Prophets of God.
3. WE BELIEVE in the truth of the Bible, but we believe that it has been tampered with and must be reinterpreted so that mankind will not be snared by the falsehoods that have been added to it.
4. WE BELIEVE in Allah's Prophets and the Scriptures they brought to the people.
5. WE BELIEVE in the resurrection of the dead – not in physical resurrection – but in mental resurrection. We believe that the so-called Negroes are most in need of mental resurrection; therefore they will be resurrected first. Furthermore, we believe we are

the people of God's choice, as it has been written, that God would choose the rejected and the despised. We can find no other persons fitting this description in these last days more than the so-called Negroes in America. We believe in the resurrection of the righteous.

6. WE BELIEVE in the judgement; we believe this first judgement will take place as God revealed, in America …
7. WE BELIEVE this is the time in history for the separation of the so-called Negroes and the so-called white Americans. We believe the Black man should be freed in name as well as in fact. By this we mean that he should be freed from the names imposed upon him by his former slave masters. Names which identified him as being the slave master's slave. We believe that if we are free indeed, we should go in our own people's names – the Black people of the Earth.
8. WE BELIEVE in justice for all, whether in God or not; we believe as others, that we are due equal justice as human beings. We believe in equality – as a nation – of equals. We do not believe that we are equal with our slave masters in the status of "freed slaves." We recognize and respect American citizens and independent peoples and we respect their laws which govern this nation.
9. WE BELIEVE that the offer of integration is hypocritical and is made by those who are trying to deceive the Black peoples into believing that their 400-year-old open enemies of freedom, justice and equality are, all of a sudden, their "friends." Furthermore, we believe that such deception is intended to prevent

Black people from realizing that the time in history has arrived for the separation from the whites of this nation. If the white people are truthful about their professed friendship toward the so-called Negro, they can prove it by dividing up America with their slaves. We do not believe that America will ever be able to furnish enough jobs for her own millions of unemployed, in addition to jobs for the 20,000,000 Black people as well.

10. WE BELIEVE that we who declare ourselves to be righteous Muslims, should not participate in wars which take the lives of humans. We do not believe this nation should force us to take part in such wars, for we have nothing to gain from it unless America agrees to give us the necessary territory wherein we may have something to fight for.
11. WE BELIEVE our women should be respected and protected as the women of other nationalities are respected and protected.
12. WE BELIEVE that Allah (God) appeared in the Person of Master W. Fard Muhammad, July 1930; the long-awaited "Messiah" of the Christians and the "Mahdi" of the Muslims. We believe further and lastly that Allah is God and besides HIM there is no God and He will bring about a universal government of peace wherein we all can live in peace together.

What Muslims Want

This is the question asked most frequently by both the whites and the Blacks. The answers to this question I shall state as simply as possible.

1. We want freedom. We want a full and complete freedom.
2. We want justice. Equal justice under the law. We want justice applied equally to all, regardless of creed or class or color.
3. We want equality of opportunity. We want equal membership in society with the best in civilized society.
4. We want our people in America whose parents or grandparents were descendants from slaves, to be allowed to establish a separate state or territory of their own – either on this continent or elsewhere. We believe that our former slave masters are obligated to provide such land and that the area must be fertile and minerally rich. We believe that our former slave masters are obligated to maintain and supply our needs in this separate territory for the next 20 to 25 years – until we are able to produce and supply our own needs. Since we cannot get along with them in peace and equality, after giving them 400 years of our sweat and blood and receiving in return some of the worst treatment human beings have ever experienced, we believe our contributions to this land and the suffering forced upon us by white America, justifies our demand for complete separation in a state or territory of our own.
5. We want freedom for all Believers of Islam now held in federal prisons. We want freedom for all Black men and women now under death sentence in innumerable prisons in the North as well as the South. We want every Black man and woman to have the freedom to accept or reject being separated from the slave master's children and establish a land of their own. We

know that the above plan for the solution of the Black and white conflict is the best and only answer to the problem between two people.

6. We want an immediate end to the police brutality and mob attacks against the so-called Negro throughout the United States. We believe that the Federal government should intercede to see that Black men and women tried in white courts receive justice in accordance with the laws of the land – or allow us to build a new nation for ourselves, dedicated to justice, freedom and liberty.
7. As long as we are not allowed to establish a state or territory of our own, we demand not only equal justice under the laws of the United States, but equal employment opportunities – NOW! We do not believe that after 400 years of free or nearly free labor, sweat and blood, which has helped America become rich and powerful, that so many thousand of Black people should have to subsist on relief, charity or live in poor houses.
8. We want the government of the United States to exempt our people from ALL taxation as long as we are deprived of equal justice under the laws of the land.
9. We want equal education – but separate schools up to 16 for boys and 18 for girls on the condition that the girls be sent to women's colleges and universities. We want all Black children educated, taught and trained by their own teachers. Under such [a] schooling system we believe we will make a better nation of people. The United States government should provide, free, all necessary text books and equipment, schools and college buildings. The Muslim teachers shall be left free to teach and train their people in the way of righteousness, decency and self respect.

10. We believe that intermarriage or race mixing should be prohibited. We want the religion of Islam taught without hindrance or suppression.

These are some of the things that we, the Muslims, want for our people in North America.

(Muhammad, *Message*, 161–164)

Most of the declarations of "What Muslims Believe" are not unexpected given Elijah Muhammad's formulation of Islam. The major aspects of his understanding of the five principles appear therein. However, the demands for the United States to be divided, the non-participation in its wars, and the protection of black women are more unexpected. The issues of imprisonment, police brutality, taxation, education, and intermarriage addressed within "What Muslims Want" seem to depart from purely religious issues into socio-economic and political ones. His formulation of Islam cannot, however, be separated from these other programs. As noted earlier, merely to focus on the five pillars and the five principles is to assume the framework of a normative Islam and to essentialize Islam. Nor would he be the first Muslim to see Islam within a larger socio-economic and political framework. For him, "Allah's greatest teaching and warning to us (the so-called Negro) is: *Be Yourself!*" (Muhammad, *The Supreme Wisdom*, 12), and his Islam teaches justice, freedom, and equality. Thus, economic, political, and social reforms are just as much part of Islam as prayer.

Elijah Muhammad's dedication to promulgating these reforms for four decades despite imprisonment, persecution, and ridicule was only possible because of his honest and fervent belief in Allah – both the one he had met in person and the one in the Qur'an – and his conviction that this Allah had specifically commissioned him to bring African Americans back to their original religion, Islam. As described above, his Islam was not one whose rewards came in the hereafter, but in the here and now. It was an Islam that would free African Americans from the religious, social, economic, and political corruption of whites and prepare them for the coming Fall of America. Thus these other agendas were not separable from Islam. Nor were they for his followers in the Nation of Islam, for like the other beliefs and practices, they also came from Allah via his messenger.

DO FOR SELF: ECONOMIC SELF-SUFFICIENCY

Garvey had urged all Africans and their descendants to unite and, because of historic and contemporary racial oppression, put their race first. One of the tangible manifestations of that position was his economic program, the key feature of which was self-reliance, as demonstrated with the U.N.I.A.'s restaurants, grocery stores, and shipping line. The program was later adopted wholesale by Elijah Muhammad under the slogan "do for self." As noted earlier, his time in prison may also have helped, for he followed some of the agricultural practices employed by the prison. Even prior to his release after World War II, he had his followers pool their financial resources in order to purchase a farm. The restaurant, grocery store, bakery, and dry cleaners followed soon thereafter.

Elijah Muhammad sought nothing less than the establishment of an independent African American economy – the most tangible expression of his "do for self" precept. In his "Program for Self-Development" in *Message to the Blackman*, he stated that African Americans have been charmed by the luxury of the slave-master so that they could not even see the opportunities before them. Blame lies with the wickedness of whites and the laziness of blacks. Oddly enough, his models were other nations, including the United States, which he normally criticized:

> The good things of this earth could be theirs if they would only unite and acquire wealth as the masters and other independent nations have. The Negroes could have all this if they could get up and go to work for self. They are far too lazy as a Nation – 100 years up from slavery and still looking to the master to care for them and give them a job, bread and a house to live in on the master's land. You should be ashamed of yourselves, surely the white race has been very good in the way of making jobs for their willing slaves, but this cannot go on forever; we are about at the end of it and do something for SELF or else.
>
> (Muhammad, *Message*, 170)

He even stated that the "slave-master" had given African Americans an education but that they refuse to use it "for self." He urged, "We must become an independent people."

The road to that black independence involved separation from whites: religiously, politically, socially, and economically. African Americans were told to pool their financial and physical resources, their education, and their skills. Elijah Muhammad suggested, for example, that if a few Muslims had experience in the grocery business, they should join forces to open their own grocery store. African Americans had to build their own homes, schools, hospitals, and factories. Also, African Americans should make their neighborhoods decent places to live, patronize only African American owned and operated businesses, and boycott white businesses if possible. This was the mark of a "true Muslim." He also encouraged his followers to focus on purchasing their own homes, and until they did, they had no business buying expensive cars and clothes. If possible, they should buy farmland to grow their own food, or timberland. Certainly Elijah Muhammad achieved great economic success and served as a model for how African Americans could improve their socioeconomic status. As we will see, by the mid-1970s the socioeconomic status of many members of the Nation of Islam had in fact changed as a result of his plan and, as a result, their worldviews began to change too.

The Nation of Islam implemented this economic program to demonstrate that its aims could be achieved. It already had farms, homes, schools, and businesses. Elijah Muhammad encouraged African Americans to commit to paying five cents per day to an "Economic Savings Program" to combat unemployment, poor housing, and hunger (and nakedness) among African Americans. He also encouraged readers of *Message to the Blackman* to send quarters every week to his Chicago mosque. He would collect this money until he had a million dollars, and then use it to begin to build an independent banking system. The ultimate goal, however, was to raise five hundred million dollars. If his followers simply forwent alcohol, cigarettes, drugs, fine automobiles, dozens of dresses for women, and so forth, money could be pooled rapidly. He was very specific. He asked for three years of sacrifice: men should have no more than three suits, none costing more than sixty-five dollars, and only a few pairs of shoes, none of which should cost over sixteen dollars.

The line between Elijah Muhammad's economic program and his religion was clearly blurred for him. Having been called a "black capitalist," he responded by arguing, "whatever I'm doing has nothing whatsoever to do with this 'ism' or that 'ism' or any kind of 'ism' … My work is all in the line of what Allah, the Almighty God, Who Came in the person of Master W. Fard Muhammad, to Whom praises are due forever, specifically assigned me to do" (Ghareeb, 15). Elsewhere he stated that: "The Black man in America faces a serious economic problem today and the white race's Christianity cannot solve it. You, the so-called Negro, with the help of Allah can solve your own problem" (Muhammad, *Message*, 173). Even his specific three-year Economic Savings Program was set up "according to the Divine Supreme Being and His Prophets." His economic goals were inextricably intertwined with his formulation of Islam. It is also clear, however, that his economic program never deviated from Western capitalism. He simply sought to create an independent, black capitalist society – one whose measures of success were wealth and property. In that sense, it was not a radical program, but a conservative one. That he was not offering something fundamentally new is evident when he advised his readers: "Observe the operations of the white man. He is successful. He makes no excuse for his failures. He works hard in a collective manner. You do the same" (Muhammad, *Message*, 174).

A LAND OF OUR OWN: SEPARATION, NOT INTEGRATION

Elijah Muhammad, like Drew Ali before him, drew on the secular black nationalism of Garvey. Garvey's "back to Africa" program was re-envisioned by Drew Ali and Elijah Muhammad as a religious return to the continent, not a physical one. However, Elijah Muhammad did have a physical component that Drew Ali did not; African Americans should live apart from white Americans in a separate nation.

Elijah Muhammad had always objected to integration of the races – a position that clearly put him at odds with the civil rights movement of Martin Luther King, Jr. His early writings from the late 1950s and early 1960s simply discouraged racial mixing in schools and churches, and particularly through intermarriage and the "mingling of blood." This period in time was to be the time of the great separation of blacks and whites, in preparation for the Judgment Day and the Fall of America. By the time of the publication of *The Supreme Wisdom: Volume Two*, he had begun to call for a more distinct political separation: "We CAN and WILL live without the white race to rule us, as we did for millions of years before the devil's appearance on our planet" (Muhammad, *The Supreme Wisdom: Volume Two*, 24). Though he provided no specifics, he stated that he wanted to see his people in a country that they could call their own. However, he primarily still focused on economic independence, which was exemplified in the farms, forested land, factories, textile mills, stores, bakeries, warehouses, and so forth that were needed to produce everything to meet their own needs. But this independence was also a necessary first step to political independence.

By the mid-1960s, Elijah Muhammad had developed his position, calling not merely for political independence but political separation *in land carved out of the United States*. In *Message to the Blackman*, in a section entitled "Land of Our Own and Qualifications," he outlined his vision and made his case to African Americans. For the latter, he argued that, what prevents black independence is a lack of knowledge of self, of God, of the devil, and of true religion. The long-term goal was self-pride, self-independence, and a desire for a country and a government "of our own under the law and justice and righteousness for every one of our poor black people throughout the world" (Muhammad, *Message*, 220). But the place to start was the United States, where he felt that African Americans were dependent on whites for jobs, education, and food. Continued integration was merely a form of self-destruction, and no nation could succeed while in "the house of the enemy."

To build his nation, Elijah Muhammad felt that "his 22 million" people needed land. Whites must divide part of the United States between African Americans, who as slaves helped build the land for three hundred years, and American Indians, who were robbed of their land five hundred years ago. Several states with fertile land and minerals would suffice. There were already among these twenty-two million sufficient engineers, scientists, educators, farmers, and so forth to construct a government.

While the goal was to be entirely self-sufficient, he also recognized that they would need support for twenty to twenty-five years from other independent black peoples outside of the United States. In the declaration cited above, he made it clear that the United States should also assist by way of reparations. In any case, whites had no claim to the land or even the Earth: there were only "400 million white people on our planet earth. Our population runs into billions, and the earth belongs to us. We are the original owners of the earth and will take it and rule it again. This is the time" (Muhammad, *Message*, 233).

To distinguish these elements of Elijah Muhammad's teachings as belonging to his "politics" or to his "religion" does not reflect how he understood either category: "Indeed, politics and religion were wedded in fascinating and problematical ways within the movement" (Curtis, *Islam in Black America*, 2). Once again, viewing Islam as a religion fundamentally devoid of politics essentializes it and puts the scholar in the position of judging what constitutes true Islam. And certainly Elijah Muhammad saw its political program as part of his religion: the program itself was given to him by Allah. Because of its divine origin, it was not only possible, but also inevitable. Nor was this merely an insignificant part of his Islam. He boldy insisted that it is "far more important to teach the separation of Blacks and Whites in America than prayer" (Muhammad, *Message*, 204).

Politically, he was a racial separatist, arguing for segregation and demanding that African Americans be given several states within the continental United States for their own independent and separate territory. His model was the modern nation-state. Moreover, here too one can see that he was not offering a radically new approach to racial issues: "If you were forced to choose between segregation and integration you would be better off to ask the southern white people to give segregation back to you" (Muhammad, "The Fatal Mistake," 17). Furthermore, though his rhetoric advocated activism, his explicit restrictions on his followers enforced quietism. This approach was therefore thoroughly conservative: it did little to physically challenge the status quo in the United States – much to the chagrin of some of his followers, including Malcolm X.

PROTECT YOUR WOMEN!

The Supreme Wisdom contained almost no material addressing women's issues. Chapter 14 of *The Supreme Wisdom: Volume Two* is dedicated to the subject of women under headings such as "We Must Change Our Women's Present Condition," "Our Men Are to Blame for the Women's Condition," "Protect Your Women!," "Protection of Our Women Is Imperative," and "Practical Steps for the Safeguard of Our Women." *Message to the Blackman* further developed these themes, indicating that Elijah Muhammad became increasingly concerned about the lifestyles of African American women, and what *men* should do about them.

Elijah Muhammad argued that no "nation" had less respect and less control of their women than the so-called Negroes in America. Obviously, he was addressing men primarily. The specific issues that concerned him included: "Our women are allowed to walk and stay in the streets all night long, with any strange men that they desire." They frequent taverns and dance halls and, as a result, "fill *our* homes with children who are *other than our own* – children who are often fathered by the devil himself." Moreover, by cavorting with white men, black women filled themselves and black men with social (that is, sexually transmitted) diseases. His patriarchal position was made explicit when he asked, "Who is to blame for her condition? It is YOU MEN who are to blame, not women. It is you, the men and not women who are the heads of your families" (Muhammad,

The Supreme Wisdom: Volume Two, 56–57). However, white males impregnating black women was not the only problem. He argued that blacks who desired white women hated themselves and their own kind.

Elijah Muhammad's remedy included, not surprisingly, not permitting wives and daughters to mix with white men or even "strange men." He went so far as to insist, "Stop allowing the white men to shake hands or speak to your women anytime and anywhere" (Muhammad, *Message*, 171). More surprising was his demand that women not try to appear white: bleaching, powdering, and coloring hair, using lipstick and other makeup, wearing shorts, and "going half-nude" in public were prohibited. Women should not go to swimming pools or the beach with men, but only to pools that were for women only. Women must also be prevented from using unclean language, smoking, and using drugs. As for socializing, he demanded, "Stop your women from going into bars and taverns and sitting and drinking with men and strangers. Stop them from sitting in those places with *anyone*, for they shouldn't even *be* there" (Muhammad, *The Supreme Wisdom: Volume Two*, 58). To further his reform program for African American women, all temples ran weekly classes in Muslim Girl's Training and General Civilization. The purpose of these classes was for women to "learn their special duties and responsibilities as future wives and mothers" (Muhammad, *The Supreme Wisdom: Volume Two*, 58). Women were important, no doubt, but their roles were to be wives and mothers. That is to say, their roles were ones that valued them only in relation to men.

The importance of motherhood for African American women was evident also in Elijah Muhammad's vehement opposition to birth control. He taught that birth control was a plot by the white devils to eliminate the black race, just as Mr. Yakub had done six millennia earlier. Using birth control was also a sin against Allah, a sin that He would punish on

Judgment Day. Moreover, in the course of this tirade against birth control, Elijah Muhammad asks, "Who wants a sterile woman?" (Muhammad, *Message*, 64).

Elijah Muhammad also attempted to enforce sartorial control over women. Women's clothing that showed too much skin, including sleeveless dresses or dresses with a hemline above the knee, were attempts by the white devil to once again strip the black woman naked. This is an old trick, for "the Children of Adam" of Qur'an 7:27 are accused of pulling off their clothing. Adam, for Elijah Muhammad, is the first white man. Dresses should ideally go at least half-way down the calf, for this was both more modest and more attractive to men. Ideally, women should opt for the full-length robes and headgear that he had designed. He preferred their long dresses to be white, green, or red, since that had been Fard Muhammad's preference. Traditional African clothing and headpieces that had become popular in the 1960s were forbidden. Wearing them could lead to expulsion from the Nation of Islam. In what seems to be a reference to the practice of veiling and seclusion by some Muslims, Elijah Muhammad wrote: "We veiled and even locked our black women in, to keep the devils' blue eyes from feasting on their beauty" (Muhammad, *The Supreme Wisdom: Volume Two*, 25). Oddly, to bolster his position he did not employ Qur'an 24:31, which also commands modesty from women.

These restrictions on women were tied directly to Elijah Muhammad's formulation of Islam, not merely a tangential issue for him. He stated that the only way to solve these problems that concerned women was to control and protect them through Islam and the Nation of Islam; women could not be protected as long as one belonged to the false religion of Christianity. Not only did he try to enforce modest dress and attempt to organize patriarchal families in which women should be protected and controlled by their fathers and husbands, but he also meted out harsh penalties for sexual infractions for both men and women. These policies certainly addressed some of the social ills as he saw them, but they also reveal his social conservatism.

BE YOURSELF! BLACK PRIDE

Along with his economic programs and political agenda, Elijah Muhammad sought to solve the problem of racism and inequality in the United States with an emphasis on black pride. As Claude Andrew Clegg III argues:

> No other historical personality has had the kind of prolonged impact on black consciousness that he has had, and no recent group in the African-American community has promoted – largely by example – economic self-help, cultural regeneration (or redefinition), and moral living more vigorously than his Nation of Islam. The Muslims were "black" long before it became fashionable to be labeled as such, and the Black Power Movement and all subsequent African-American protest styles, from the rhymes of the nationalistic rap group Public Enemy to the raison d'être of the Million Man March, are undeniably offshoots of the legacy of Elijah Muhammad.
>
> (Clegg, 282)

Black pride involved psychological, economic, political, and sociological self-transformation, all of which were hallmarks of Elijah Muhammad and his message. His means for doing so was to equate power with blackness and to demand black unity.

"God said: *Accept your own*. It is an act of intelligence and love for us to accept our own" (Muhammad, *Message*, 50). For African Americans to accept their own, they must first and foremost accept their true God, Allah, and their true religion, Islam. Once they had done that, they would accept black humanity as their true family, unite with them and reject the white race.

Whites, Elijah Muhammad argued, were devils who, despite the end of slavery, remained the enemy. They continued to mistreat African Americans, denying them equality, freedom, and justice. The practical application of this acceptance included his economic plan, his political agenda, and his efforts to stop racial intermingling (primarily by controlling women).

The racial mythology also played an important role in the psychological self-transformation involved in black pride. God was a black god. Original humanity was black humanity. Original civilization was black civilization. God was not a being who had blonde hair and blue eyes, who thus looked like (stereotypical) Europeans and their descendants in the United States. Whites were created in the image of God only insofar as they were created in the image of the original black humanity. And white, Western civilization hardly deserved the name civilization, for it was responsible for war, oppression, slavery, and murder. Only black civilization merited being described as "civilized." The story of ancient humanity and the Tribe of Shabazz to the time of Mr. Yakub furthered this reversal. It gave African Americans a noble ancestry, replacing their purported origins as uncivilized, heathen savages plucked from the jungles of Africa. By making this argument, Elijah Muhammad turned on its head the white supremacist argument. A prime example of this kind of reversal can also be seen in his treatment of the white racist claim that Africans are more closely related to other primates from which humanity evolved. He claimed that Allah had taught him that some whites had tried to "graft themselves back into the black nation." They only got as far as turning themselves into gorillas: "In fact, all the monkey family are from this 2,000 year history of the white race in Europe" (Muhammad, *Message*, 119). More important, however, was the assertion that the socio-economic ills of African Americans were not their fault; they were not lazier, less civilized, or less intelligent. These ills were the fault of white oppression.

A similar emphasis on black pride, or at least the erasure of black "shame," motivated Fard Muhammad's and later Elijah Muhammad's focus on names. This applies to collective names such as "nigger" and "Negro." The latter never used the former except to highlight white wickedness, and the latter was only employed in the expression "so-called Negro." He preferred black or black man, the Tribe of Shabazz, original man, or Asiatic, depending on the context. But this also applied to an individual's name. African Americans had white names, the names of their ancestors' slave-owners. These names bound them psychologically to the white race, keeping them "blind, deaf, and dumb" to their previous and natural religion, civilization, and way of life. He argued, therefore, that they should blot out these slave-names with an "X," which also indicated that their true African/Islamic names were unknown. By becoming Muslims, this situation would be rectified, for "one of the reasons Almighty Allah has come among us … is to give us His Names, the Most Holy and Righteous Names of the Planet Earth" (Muhammad, *Message*, 55). Allah's greatest teaching, according to Elijah Muhammad, was "Be yourself!"

Given Elijah Muhammad's formulation of Islam, it is hardly surprising that he emphasized connections with Africa far more than the Islamic links, or even the original Asiatic links. Islamic connections were important in the late 1950s and early 1960s for reasons of legitimacy, and in the late 1970s for reasons of finances. But he made clear that racial affinity trumped religious affiliation: "The Black African, the Aboriginal Black People of the earth, are our real brothers. We are part of, and belong to each other" (Muhammad, "Black Man of U.S.A. and Africa," 20). In particular, he often used the example of African countries that were fighting for or had won independence from their European colonial masters. Muslim Arabs, Pakistanis, Indonesians, and so forth mattered too, but then they too were merely the copper-colored, brown, yellow, or red variations of black. By basing racial categories on color, he was again reversing white racist categories. Instead of using white as the norm and thus classifying every other shade of skin as "colored," he used black as the norm and included every other shade of skin in that category that was "non-white." Obviously, both racial categorizations resulted in dividing humanity in exactly the same way: white and black (or colored).

Advocating this black identity by emphasizing connections between African Americans and Africans did not mean accepting African culture. Given Elijah Muhammad's fairly simplistic reversal of racial categories, it should come as no surprise that he retained many stereotypes and prejudices inherent in white racism with respect to Africa and Africans. For instance, he saw Africa as a mere extension of Asia; blacks were Asiatics, not Africans. Moreover, he considered Africa uncivilized and, except for the Christians and Muslims, full of naked jungle dwellers; and he likened African American women who dressed immodestly (by his definition) to "wild game of the jungle." More tellingly, he warned his female followers that he opposed "adopting the African dress and hair styles … accepting traditional African tribal styles and garments with gay colors" (Muhammad, "Warning to M.G.T. and G.C. Class," 4).

His opposition to African culture applied to men as well. Beards, Afros, and traditional African "garb" were dismissed as "jungle styles." He said: "I am against wearing beards. I am against men wearing long hair like women." His main issue with beards and long hair, besides being "non-modern," was hygiene. He believed them to be "germ-carriers" and unsanitary, and connected these unhygienic practices with Africa. He said that even the "white man" – who "came out of the cave … full of hair … [that] covered his whole body and face" – shaves (Muhammad, "Beards," 5). Beards or "hair worn down their backs like a woman," he added elsewhere: "This is the way the uncivilized white man went in the days when they lived in caves. It is the style of Black people of uncultured parts of Africa and the Islands of the Pacific, which was caused by the absence of the right guide, but they too will turn to the civilized way when they have the right guide" (Muhammad, "To the Black Woman in America," 16–17). And, after encouraging the "Black Man" to "wash and be clean," to refrain from using "filthy language" and from being loud, and to give up smoking, drinking, and drugs, he stated, "We must even teach Africa, and all other Black peoples, wherever they are on the earth, to have higher morals and more self-respect. We must get to them." After all, "The devil practices good manners. Why do not you and I do the same thing?" (Muhammad, "Wash and be Clean," 21).

To be fair, Elijah Muhammad had an abiding interest in hygiene. In the mid-1960s he wrote of establishing a Committee of Cleanliness that would teach and force African Americans to be clean – such a committee was already in place for Muslims. This new committee would focus on compelling African Americans to maintain the cleanliness of their bodies, clothes, and homes. Even if one owned but one suit of clothing, it should be washed and pressed each night. If one could not afford the barber, then men must trim each other's hair, and men must shave themselves so as to "look like men" (Muhammad, *Message*, 192).

Elijah Muhammad's conservative, perhaps even prejudiced, attitudes toward Africans extended to Native Americans, even though he considered them to be the red descendants of "an old Ancient People, the Black Man of Asia." Perhaps because he was unfamiliar with Christopher Columbus's error, or perhaps based on the name he made the same error in reverse: he taught that the indigenous peoples of North America originated in India, and were therefore "so-called American Indians." In a myth that seems to have much in common with early Mormon teaching, Native Americans were said to have come to the Americas because they had been exiled from India for their unbelief in Allah and refusal to worship in His religion, Islam. After reaching America on foot (as part of their punishment) via the Bering Strait, they worshiped gods that they had fashioned themselves (as they had done in India). Their almost complete annihilation by the white Europeans in the last five hundred years was a punishment for this latest rejection of Allah. With this in mind, Elijah Muhammad reached out to Native Americans with an offer: "So if you desire to live, my once-brothers, the Indians of America, seek me and I will Seek God for you, that you may live, yet again. Allah taught me that we can get along with the Indians of America, for they yet have some blood of the aboriginal Black people" (Muhammad, "Indians in America," 20).

Elijah Muhammad's economic, political, and social agendas were in many ways radical. They were radical with respect to other formulations of Islam. They were radical in overturning, often reversing the rhetoric of white supremacists. They were radical in their demands when compared to the civil rights movement. They were even radical as solutions to the various socio-economic ills that plagued many African Americans. Nevertheless, Elijah Muhammad was also conservative: economically a capitalist, politically a separatist, socially a patriarchalist, and culturally an advocate of Western cultural norms and prejudices.

6

THE TEXTUAL SOURCES OF ISLAM

Elijah Muhammad described himself as the Apostle of Allah, the Messenger of Allah, and the Prophet of Allah. Unlike Drew Ali, he never claimed to bring a new scripture from Allah. Although he conveyed Allah's supreme wisdom to his followers, he read, cited, analyzed, and interpreted many of the main textual sources employed by Muslims. He never used terms such as *'ālim* or *mufassir* for himself. And no one claims that he had the training in the Qur'an, *tafsir*, hadith, sira, *fiqh*, or Arabic that would have justified such titles. That his formulation of Islam differed so much from others who used the same texts is largely a product of his understanding of the function of scripture, and particularly the Qur'an (that is, as prophecy), and his hermeneutical approach (that is, his racialist reading). It is also due to his reading of the Qur'an in isolation from the other textual sources of Islam. For him, the sira and Sunna had no scriptural or authoritative value.

THE SIRA

Given the significance of Muhammad to Elijah Muhammad (which will be discussed below), it is somewhat surprising that in the many books and hundreds of columns that Elijah Muhammad wrote and in the speeches that he gave, there is no significant sustained narrative about Muhammad. He did know some rudimentary details found in the sira: Muhammad was an illiterate Arab born in the seventh century, who died at the age of sixty-two; and the Qur'an was revealed to him in Arabic during the month of Ramadan. He also noted that Muhammad had faced opposition in Mecca and that Arabia converted to Islam in his lifetime.

Elijah Muhammad discussed only two events from the sira at any length. The first he discussed fairly often. He found symbolic meaning in the story of Ka'ba's renovation after a fire, during which the black stone had to be removed in order to effect repairs to the shrine. The leaders of the various clans of the Quraysh argued about who should have the honor of replacing it when the repairs had been completed. Finally they agreed to allow the next man to walk through the gate to make the decision. It was Muhammad (about five years before his first revelation). In his wisdom, he had the black stone placed on a cloth that each of the clan leaders could help lift, though Muhammad set the stone in place. Elijah Muhammad's telling of the story is not much different: Muhammad found the stone out of its place and diplomatically invited the four chiefs "from four divisions to come forward and take hold of each corner of the mantle and lift it into its place, and Muhammad with His own hands who guided it into its place." But he changed the symbolism of the story: the stone symbolized African Americans; blacks from the "four points of our compass" should work together to "help raise us, their dead brothers, and put us back into our own place, in our own nation among our own people in our own native land" (Muhammad, *The Supreme Wisdom: Volume Two*, 76).

The second and more important event that Elijah Muhammad discussed was the revelation of the Qur'an and its commemoration by fasting during the month of Ramadan. He encouraged his followers to fast regularly for health reasons. As noted earlier, he also instituted a month-long fast during December. His goal was to focus his followers' minds on Fard Muhammad instead of the ubiquitous Christmas celebrations of the month, celebrations that he insisted his followers avoid. Not unexpectedly, his very atypical fast drew rebukes from other Muslims. Only a few months later, after publishing his response (below), he would adopt the typical Ramadan fast. However, his initial response was to argue that his fast made more sense:

> IN the case of the Orthodox Muslims worshipping Ramadan by not eating until after sunset, and darkness approaches (then they can eat all night long if they want to, until the next morning at dawn) – they call this a FAST!
>
> THEY say that they do this in the Month of Ramadan because Ramadan is the month in which the Holy Quran was revealed to Muhammad.
>
> BUT, the way I understand scripture, it teaches us that Muhammad received the Holy Quran over a period of twenty-three (23) years.
>
> MUHAMMAD did not receive the Holy Quran in one night or in one day. And, if he received the whole Holy Qur'an in the month of Ramadan, WHY FAST in that month?
>
> IF we are given what we want (Holy Qur'an) in that month, without FASTING, I cannot understand why we should FAST in the month of Ramadan, for the first revelation of the Holy Qur'an was already given in that month, without FASTING.
>
> IT would look more proper for us to be rejoicing over the great salvation (Holy Qur'an) that Allah (God) sent to us, in the month of Ramadan.
>
> (Muhammad, "Opposition," 16)

In the remainder of this passage, he reiterated his points: fasting is an act of sorrow, but one should rejoice at the revelation of the Qur'an. Moreover, the purpose of fasting is to receive something from Allah, but that something (in this case the Qur'an) was given without fasting. Thus it made no sense to him that Muslims would then commemorate the event in this fashion. His habit of selective reading of the Qur'an is evident on this issue too. Elsewhere he had cited and discussed Qur'an 2:185, which explicitly enjoins fasting in Ramadan *because* it was the month in which the Qur'an was revealed. This apropos verse is not adduced here.

In any case, it seems clear that Elijah Muhammad did not have a copy of the sira that he could consult. Had he possessed one, it is doubtful whether he would have had any use for it. These few details of Muhammad's life in which he expressed any interest, he took from his edition of the Qur'an. The translator, Maulana Muhammad Ali, had provided it with a substantial introduction that discussed the biography of Muhammad in some detail. Elijah Muhammad thought most of it insignificant.

THE SUNNA

Something similar could be said about the Sunna. The *Sahīhs* of al-Bukharī and Muslim were not on his bookshelf. The words Sunna or hadith never appear in his writings or speeches. Only once did he cite a hadith: "According to the Holy Qur-an (30:30), one of the greatest teachings of brotherhood is laid down by us by the Prophet Muhammad in these words: 'A Muslim is not a Muslim until he loves for his brother what he loves for himself'" (Muhammad, *Message*, 79). It is uncertain why he associated this hadith with this verse. Muhammad Ali and Yusuf Ali, the translators of the Qur'an whom he employed, did not cite it in their discussions of the verse. It is, however, a well-known hadith, for it is recorded by al-Bukhārī, Muslim, and Nawawī, but the most common English translation begins, "None of you believes ..." Perhaps most intriguing is that Elijah Muhammad seems to have conflated the qur'anic verse with a statement by Muhammad.

A similar phenomenon occurred in one of Elijah Muhammad's exhortations to prayer, discussed in chapter 4. He cited six verses of the Qur'an. These he took directly from Ahmad Ghalwash's second volume of *The Religion of Islam* (without attribution). He then skipped three of Ghalwash's paragraphs on the necessity of prayer in Arabic and ablution, but continued with Ghalwash's seven statements about prayer by Muhammad. Again, Elijah Muhammad did not identify them as hadiths. In fact, in the context of his redaction of the passage, the reader could have easily assumed that they were passages from the Qur'an itself. However, he must have known they were not, given that Ghalwash's preceding paragraph identified these hadiths as such.

THE QUR'AN

In marked contrast to the sira and the Sunna, the Qur'an is ubiquitous in the writings of Elijah Muhammad. Its importance to him has already been discussed. Fard Muhammad is said to have taught directly from an Arabic Qur'an, and had provided him with several Qur'ans, at least one in Arabic and two English translations. In 1934, Elijah Muhammad was already citing the Qur'an in his publications. Such was his early attachment to it that, while in prison during World War II, his wife copied out verses from the Qur'an and sent them to him. He repeatedly encouraged his followers to own, read, respect, understand, and teach it. And, although he was dependent on English translations, he encouraged his followers and his sons, especially Wallace and Akbar, to read the Qur'an in Arabic. None of this is surprising, for he thought of himself as a Muslim and the scripture of Islam was the Qur'an.

His African American followers were, however, far more familiar with the Bible than they were with the Qur'an. They were thus largely dependent on Elijah Muhammad for the interpretation of the scripture that he had introduced to them. In fact, when they were confused about what it said, they were encouraged to ask him rather than engage in independent exegesis. This was his role as Allah's messenger. When his reading of the Qur'an from a racial and contemporary perspective was challenged, he even retorted, "The Last Messenger is given a complete understanding and interpretation of the Holy Qur-an. He does not have to read the entire book. You don't have to read the Holy Qur-an to me – just show me what you don't understand about it" (Muhammad, "From Savior's Day," 10).

One could, therefore, see Elijah Muhammad as *mufassir*, though he never employed the term. He certainly adopted the role of official interpreter of the Qur'an and the Bible for his followers. In his various writings, the Bible is cited roughly twice as often as the Qur'an, but he would not be the first *mufassir* to have given significant attention to materials drawn from Jewish and Christian sources – though he undoubtedly had not even heard of the term *Isrā'īlīyāt*. His topics of interest also ranged far beyond those of a typical *mufassir*. Columns in *Muhammad Speaks* and many chapters within his *Message to the Blackman* might not normally be understood as "religious." These include his aforementioned political program of separation of blacks and whites, his economic program of self-sufficiency for blacks, and his demand for a separate homeland within the continental United States for blacks. Not unexpectedly, he draws on virtually no qur'anic or biblical material to support these teachings. What ties together his political agenda and the more religious teachings (as outlined in the previous two chapters) is the hegemony of his racial myth of origins and racial eschatology. Yet here too, having a preconceived understanding of Islam that shapes the interpretation of the Qur'an is not atypical of *mufassirs*. Only the content of that understanding, for him, is atypical.

Elijah Muhammad's exegesis largely ignored most of the techniques typically employed by *mufassirs*. It is unlikely that he was even aware of such standard topics as variant readings, pre-Islamic poetry, circumstances of revelation, and abrogation. Nor, of course, did he have the facility with Arabic to engage in lexical, grammatical, or rhetorical analysis of the Qur'an. Quite often he did use identification and specification (*ta'yīn* and *tasmiya*) in the form of glosses. And his interpretations, like the sira and circumstances of revelation material, often provided a narrative framework for qur'anic verses. His narrative, however, was his racial mythology. From the discussion of the Sunna above it is clear that he did not use prophetic hadiths as part of his exegesis, unless one understands "prophetic" traditions to include material that refers to Fard Muhammad and himself. Given this apparent unfamiliarity with the Islamic exegetical tradition and deviation from it, many non-Nation of Islam Muslims would see the application of the description of *mufassir* to Elijah Muhammad as dubious.

John Wansbrough, a scholar of *tafsīr*, argued that the *Sitz im Leben* for narrative exegesis is the popular sermon and that it had a central role in the process of social identity and social formation. Elijah Muhammad's writings were similarly rooted in the popular sermon. Many of his writings are reworked sermons. And the racial mythology (from the creation of the white race of blue-eyed devils and their imminent destruction), the establishment of rituals such as prayer, and the political and economic agenda were all critical to establishing and perpetuating his Nation of Islam. Because he did so by employing qur'anic verses and Islamic terminology, from this perspective at least, he could be seen as a *mufassir*. His methodology is also not without precedent in Islam. Early Islam featured the storyteller (*qāss*; plural *qussās*). They often told stories that were paraenetic or morally edifying. These often employed biblical and qur'anic passages and wove them into tales about Muhammad. These stories, some of which obviously had no factual basis, nevertheless found their way into the sira and *tafsīr*. Thus, despite Elijah Muhammad's heterodoxy, he might also be understood as a modern-day *qāss*.

This general assessment of Elijah Muhammad's approach to the Qur'an is based on an overview of the four decades during which he wrote and spoke about the scripture. But his use of the Qur'an was not static. His use of and familiarity with the Qur'an increased significantly over time. In 1930 he had presumably never heard of the Qur'an. In 1934, he already cited a few verses. But even by the late 1950s, as evidenced in *The Supreme Wisdom*, he only employed three exegetical techniques with regard to the Qur'an: adducing qur'anic phraseology, simply citing passages, and providing limited interpretation. A good example of the former two techniques can be seen with his early references to Fard Muhammad. Elijah Muhammad rarely used his name. Instead, he simply employed the name "Allah." For example, "Allah has taught us that our foreparents were deceived and brought into America by a slave-trader whose name was John Hawkins in the year 1555"; "Allah greatly rejoiced over us and was real happy that He had found us – the lost Nation of Islam in the wilderness of North America"; and "The so-called Negroes do not need to fear any more if they will believe in Allah (God) and follow me" (Muhammad, *The Supreme Wisdom*, 15, 17, and 21). In these cases there is little doubt that he is referring to Fard Muhammad. However, when he employed qur'anic phraseology such as "I have the truth from the All-wise One, Allah, to Whom all praise is due" or "Obey Allah and his Apostle" – given the context in *The Supreme Wisdom*, he was also referring to Fard Muhammad (Muhammad, *The Supreme Wisdom*, 21 and 50). Moreover, the first passage above is contained within a paragraph in which Elijah

Muhammad defended his teaching on the birth of the white race. This technique may not appear to be exegetical, but by identifying "Allah" with Fard Muhammad, and himself with "Apostle," his followers would read the Qur'an's Allah and the Qur'an's Apostle exactly as he did. It seems unlikely that he consciously manipulated his followers to do so, since he genuinely believed Fard Muhammad to be Allah. Nevertheless, it was an extremely effective way of dictating how the Qur'an would be understood.

A very similar process took place when Elijah Muhammad simply quoted a verse or two from the Qur'an. It was the context he provided that determined how the verse would be understood. For example, speaking of the hereafter, he wrote "Here I shall quote only these beautiful verses from the Holy Quran (89:27–30): 'O soul that is at rest, return to your Lord, well-pleased with Him, well-pleasing; So enter among My servants and enter into My Paradise'"; and with regard to the religion of Islam, "Allah says of Islam in the Holy Qur'an, 'This day I have perfected for you a religion; completed my favor on you and chose for you Islam as a religion.' (Chapter 5:3)" (Muhammad, *The Supreme Wisdom*, 26 and 31). However, the first passage was preceded by two others that argued that the hereafter is now on Earth and not "a life of spirits (spooks)," and the latter by passages that speak of Islam as the "original religion of Black mankind" and the "religion of the whole tribe of Shabazz . . . [and] the religion of Yakub, the father of the white race, before his fall." Once again, the Qur'an was being framed within the context of his racial mythology and his understanding of Allah. Having done so, he could confidently encourage his followers, "Read the Scriptures carefully on the life in the Hereafter, and try to understand their true meaning, and you will find that the Hereafter isn't what you have been believing" (Muhammad, *The Supreme Wisdom*, 26).

When Elijah Muhammad provided explicit interpretation of a verse, by first citing it and then paraphrasing it, he often did so to demonstrate how a verse contains prophecy. In a pericope entitled, "Islam Will Replace All Other Religions," he cites Qur'an 61:9, "He it is who sent His Apostle with the guidance and the True religion that he may make it overcome the religions, all of them, though the polytheists may be averse." His title itself glossed "overcome" with "will replace," which recast this verse as a prophecy. (He also replaced Muhammad Ali's "Messenger" with "Apostle.") He seems to be unaware of the traditional interpretations that would regard this "overcoming" as a *fait accompli* since the first revelation of the Qur'an, and he isolated it from its qur'anic context. To make his point even more forcefully, Elijah Muhammad added, "In the above verse Allah (God) in the last days of this present world (of wicked infidels) states that He must destroy false religions with the True Religion Islam. It (Islam) must overcome all other religions" (Muhammad, *The Supreme Wisdom*, 43). Thus, this verse (like most for him in the Qur'an and the Bible) prophesies future events: those of the recent past of white rule, those of the present, or, as in this case, the imminent future. Like other ghulat, therefore, he employed an esoteric system of allegorical Qur'an interpretation. In his case, symbology was racial; his proclivity to read most scripture as prophecy about the races was not so much to elucidate the Qur'an as to substantiate his racial mythology. In this proclivity, however, he was much like Mirza Ghulam Ahmad, who also saw the stories in the Qur'an, in fact the whole Qur'an, as an ocean of prophecies.

The Supreme Wisdom: Volume 2 reproduced almost every passage in its predecessor. The role of the Qur'an in this second volume does not increase. Although the second volume is almost twice as long as the first, it only contains twelve additional references to the Qur'an. The most noticeable shift is from the many pericopes that drew on Fard Muhammad's teachings (indicated by expressions such as "Allah says") to ones that were the teachings of Elijah Muhammad himself (indicated by expressions such as "I say"). Of the twelve new citations from the Qur'an, however, it appears that he was growing increasingly fond of his third exegetical technique: citing the verse and then paraphrasing it. In so doing, he often turned them into prophecy. Surat al-Ikhlās (that is, Qur'an 112), for example, was read as a special warning for the "lost found members of the Asiatic nation" who had begun to worship gods other than Allah after their enslavement.

The style and content of *Message to the Blackman in America* (1965) is significantly different. It has thirteen main (and coherently organized) sections, each of which is composed of numerous chapters. Biblical and qur'anic verses sometimes serve as epigraphs. Nevertheless, the same techniques are employed, and the verses continue to be interpreted so as to support aspects of Elijah Muhammad's mythology. An increasing comfort and familiarity with the Qur'an is attested to by the over 200 qur'anic references in *Message to the Blackman*. Some sections are replete with such quotations, particularly those entitled "Islam," "The Devil," "Prayer Service," "Hypocrites, Disbelievers, and Obedience," and "The Judgement." Many passages in the Qur'an deal with these themes, thus it is not surprising that Elijah Muhammad availed himself of them. Just as expected is the dearth of qur'anic references in the sections on "Program and Position," "Economic Program," "Persecution of the Righteous," "Land of our Own," and "Answer to Critics."

Three features remained constant in Elijah Muhammad's interpretation of the Qur'an: he remained dependent on his English translations; he read it through the lens of Fard Muhammad's racial mythology; and, as the Apostle of Allah, he alone understood the hidden prophecies of the Qur'an (and the Bible). Initially, he simply quoted isolated verses, allowing the context or his titles to direct the reader to his interpretation. Later, he relied more on glosses and paraphrases to more clearly dictate the meaning he believed the verses held. In addition, his knowledge of the Qur'an certainly increased with time; in 1956, his knowledge of the Qur'an was described as "staggering." That was never the case, except perhaps in comparison to his followers. This is evident from his speeches. Whereas his columns and books were often littered with qur'anic verses, his speeches were not, suggesting that he did not have much of the Qur'an memorized. Nor did he display any interest in verses that would have proved problematic, such as Qur'an 5:82, which claims Christians as those closest in friendship to believers. Of the major textual sources of Islam, only the Qur'an mattered to Elijah Muhammad. Having in a sense removed it from its traditional context provided by the sira, the Sunna, and centuries of *tafsīr*, the Qur'an became pliable and easily molded to the racial mythology provided to him by Fard Muhammad.

7

OTHER MUSLIMS

Elijah Muhammad considered himself a Muslim, but many other Muslims did not. His relationships with other Muslims, that is, those Muslims not in the Nation of Islam, were complex and changed over time. The only simple relationship he had with Muslims was with members of his own Nation of Islam. He was their Apostle and they were *his* Muslims. They were expected to accept his teachings and carry out his commands. These commands could range from making donations to shunning a close friend or family member because he or she had failed to believe or obey properly. His claim to be the Apostle and his authority to lead his Muslim followers came directly from Allah himself. It was not predicated on having obedient followers, nor was it based on acceptance from non-Nation of Islam Muslims (since he himself calls these Muslims "orthodox Muslims," so shall I, though I am not suggesting they possess any doctrinal purity, priority, or normativity). He steadfastly believed that Allah himself, in the person of Wali Fard Muhammad, had appointed him to be his Apostle to the Lost-Found Nation of Islam in the wilderness of America. For over three years Fard Muhammad had mentored his protégé. Then for years he withstood persecution and imprisonment for the sake of his beliefs. His faith did not waver. Then, for the remainder of his life Allah continued to speak to him at least once a year. The only other authority he seemed to recognize, scripture in the form of both the Bible and the Qur'an, simply confirmed for him everything he had been taught by Allah about Islam, the black race, and the rise and fall of the white race. However, it is precisely this source of his authority – Allah as Fard Muhammad – that other Muslims found most objectionable.

Therefore, despite his own demand for absolute authority, Elijah Muhammad experienced significant opposition. The opposition that troubled him the most was that from those for whom he employed the term "hypocrites." These were Muslims who once belonged to the Nation of Islam. The second most problematic group were those African American Muslims from the late 1950s onwards who charged him and his followers in the Nation of Islam with not being "real Muslims." These opponents focused on the novel beliefs and practices of the Nation of Islam, and even objected to his use of the words "Muslim" and "Islam." The final group of opponents were Muslims who lived outside of the United States in countries that are predominantly Muslim, and often Arab. Initially, he viewed these outside Muslim or "orthodox Muslim" opponents as potential allies, "copper-colored" brothers who might be misguided or unaware of his unique circumstances in the United States. Later, they became "white Muslims," who were thus in league with the white devils.

HYPOCRITES

The term "hypocrite" was one that Elijah Muhammad adopted early to describe opponents who were once part of the Nation of Islam. The earliest hypocrite was his younger brother Kalot Muhammad who, along with an assistant minister named Augustus Muhammad, challenged the elder brother's leadership. They also led their own movement out of Chicago Temple

No. 2 in 1935 and forced Elijah Muhammad to flee the city. Later, he had to contend with former followers who broke ranks with him, most notably Malcolm X and two of his own sons. In Elijah Muhammad's description of these events in 1935 (see chapter 3), most of the followers, seventy-five percent to be precise, were labeled as hypocrites. The issue from his perspective was that his brother "wanted the teachings for himself." This event set the pattern for Elijah Muhammad's response to any resistance to his authority or teachings. Over three decades later his brother's betrayal still rankled, and was still being compared to the latest and greatest hypocrite, Malcolm X.

Malcolm X, when he left the Nation of Islam, became the "chief hypocrite" for Elijah Muhammad. From the subsequent propaganda campaign, it is clear that Elijah Muhammad thought that most hypocrites were traitors, motivated by a lust for power. In the case of Malcolm X, he allowed others to heap vitriol on him. A letter written by a senior official in the Nation of Islam to Malcolm X and published in *Muhammad Speaks* called him "the number one hypocrite of all time," claiming that to call him an Uncle Tom is "an insult to all other Uncle Toms on earth," and describing him as "a dog returning to his own vomit" (Shabazz, 9). The harshest and most sustained attack on Malcolm X came from Louis X (later Louis Farrakhan), who systematically critiqued all of Malcolm X's activities and went so far as to suggest that Malcolm X was worthy of death. Malcolm X's adoption of Sunni Islam was dismissed by Elijah Muhammad: "This chief hypocrite is not with Allah; if he were with Allah, he would be with me." Breaking with Elijah Muhammad meant breaking with Allah: "If he is the last of the 22 million, I shall remind him of this evil and wicked acts done to me in return for the good that I did for him. He could not have risen against me if I had not given him so much knowledge of Allah and His religion" (Muhammad, "Victory of the Apostle," 3–4).

Just as Elijah Muhammad had no hesitation in calling his brother Kalot (or his national minister) a hypocrite, he had no problem doing the same to his sons. Just after Malcolm X left the Nation of Islam, so did Elijah Muhammad's sons, Wallace and Akbar. Wallace Muhammad had had doubts about his father's teachings for many years. As he later described, while imprisoned for draft-dodging he had spent time reading the Qur'an and gradually moved toward a more Sunni understanding of Islam – what he described as the "Islam of the Qur'an." Since it was he who had confirmed to Malcolm X that the rumors about his father's infidelities were true, and since he had objected to the corruption of some Nation of Islam officials, it is not clear if his excommunication, harassment, and the elimination of financial support were due simply to his heretical beliefs. However, by responding publicly to his expulsion by revealing the Nation of Islam's darkest secrets – including adultery, alcohol consumption, and corruption – he became a hypocrite in his father's eyes. Akbar Muhammad had been studying at al-Azhar in Cairo and thus had the most firsthand experience of Sunni Islam of any significant figure in the Nation of Islam. When he returned late in 1964 and spoke to members of the Nation of Islam, *Muhammad Speaks* published the following announcement:

> On Sunday, November 26, 1964, at Muhammad's Temple No. 7 in New York City, a speech was made by Akbar Muhammad containing statements and views which were not in keeping with the teachings and principles of the Honorable Elijah Muhammad, the Messenger of Allah. It has therefore been decreed by the Messenger that Akbar Muhammad is no longer to be regard as a follower of his father in what Allah has revealed to his father in the person of Master W. F. Muhammad. Akbar is now classified as a hypocrite by his father and by all those who follow him.
>
> The Honorable Elijah Muhammad, in the tradition of all great spiritual leaders of modern and ancient times, will forever defend

> the truths entrusted to him by Almighty God, Allah, and neither kith nor kin nor defectors of Any Kind will be allowed to alter the obligation or the divine mission the Messenger is destined to accomplish for his people.
>
> ("Decree Akbar Muhammad," 9)

With Akbar it is clear that doctrinal differences alone merited the charge of hypocrisy, a charge whose punishment is expulsion.

By 1965, Elijah Muhammad felt it necessary to include a section entitled "Hypocrites, Disbelievers and Obedience" in *Message to a Blackman*. In *The Supreme Wisdom: Volume Two* the term "hypocrite" was employed in only one pericope, but it was applied to "white Christians" who, despite the Golden Rule, went so far as to kill their black co-religionists. In the later book, Elijah Muhammad most clearly identified with Muhammad. The hypocrites were those who say "he has forged it or it is of his own making." This is obviously a reference to Qur'an 10:38, 11:13, 11:35, 21:05, 25:4, 34:43, 42:24; 46:8, 52:33, 69:44, or more likely 32:3 since Elijah Muhammad explicitly argued that he, unlike Muhammad, was a warner to a people who had never before had a warner. (He claimed that Mecca had at least two prophets prior to Muhammad, Abraham and Ishmael, whereas African Americans had none.) In another description of hypocrites, he expanded the category:

> A hypocrite, regardless to where he appears or regardless to what organization he may be a member of – whether governmental hypocrite, an industrial hypocrite, a business hypocrite or a religious hypocrite – is the most unwanted and hated of all the people concerned. They are also the most hated by God. They are double-crossers; they come in claiming belief and then go out disbelieving.
>
> (Muhammad, *Message*, 255)

As was his wont on the subject of hypocrites, he supplemented his depiction with the many qur'anic verses on hypocrites. In some articles, he simply listed the verses found in the index entry on "hypocrites" in Muhammad Ali's translation of the Qur'an. Elsewhere, he wrote: "One Hypocrite among the Muslims, is worse than one hundred disbelievers who have never sought to come among the Muslims." Hypocrites are described as "evil," "poisonous," and "not only hated by Allah (God) but he is hated by all believers." He hopes Allah gives them the "fire of hell" (Muhammad, "Hypocrites!" 18).

For Elijah Muhammad, "there is no excuse for their deviation" (Muhammad, *Message*, 257). The only solution to hypocrisy was absolute obedience. Here too he preferred simply to list qur'anic verses that command Muslims to obey Allah and his messenger. Even sympathizing with hypocrites was a form of rebellion, he warned: "God is very hard on those who disobey His Messenger. He warns in his Holy Qur-an not to quarrel and dispute or raise our voices above the Messenger's voice. Strict respect and honor is demanded for His Messengers" (Muhammad, *Message*, 260).

AMERICAN MUSLIM OPPOSITION

Elijah Muhammad did not normally employ the term "hypocrite" to describe Muslims outside the Nation of Islam who opposed him. That term carried with it a sense of betrayal and was reserved for former followers. Terminology aside, he was just as vehement in his attacks on these other opponents. His model for dealing with such attacks was not his schism with his brother Kalot back in 1935, but more the slightly earlier attack by African American Christian pastors on Fard Muhammad. They had demanded proof of Fard Muhammad's prophethood and asked questions designed to confound him in front of his followers. Fard Muhammad's response had been not to meet their demands or to answer their questions, but rather to attack them personally by questioning their motives (Sahib, 85).

When Elijah Muhammad was criticized by other American Muslims, their criticisms were predictable and came from African American converts to Sunni Islam whose own movements were in direct competition with the Nation of Islam, or from Muslim immigrants from the Arab Middle East. Talib Ahmad Dawud, leader of an organization called the Muslim Brotherhood USA, was the first major critic to publicly criticize Elijah Muhammad and his formulation of Islam. The two men exchanged theological and personal barbs in popular African American newspapers. Dawud's attack focused Elijah Muhammad's claim that Allah appeared in the person of Fard Muhammad, the depiction of race as central to the teachings of Islam, the prophecy of a future book that would replace the Qur'an, and the improper prayers used by the Nation of Islam. Dawud also asserted that Fard Muhammad was a Turkish white man who was once a Nazi agent and that his messenger, Elijah Muhammad, was a "phony," an ex-convict, and a teacher of racial hatred. It was Dawud's proclamation that Elijah Muhammad was not a true Muslim and that he would be forbidden entry into Mecca that prompted Elijah Muhammad to make his *'umra* in 1959. Dawud even planned to file a lawsuit to prevent him from using the words "Islam" and "Muslim" when speaking of the Nation of Islam.

Elijah Muhammad took great umbrage over such attacks. He retorted with a personal attack on Dawud and his wife, the singer Dakota Staton:

> Talid Ahmad Dawud and his TV blues-singing Miss Dakota Staton (who the paper says is Mrs. Alijah Rabia Dawud in private life) and whom the world can hear her filthy blues and love songs and see her immodestly dressed, were successful last week in

> getting a chance to breathe their venomous poison against me and my followers in this paper and in the local Chicago paper, *The Crusader*. Mr. Dawud is from the West Indies (Antigua) and was born a British subject. He was known by the name Rannie (sounds like a devil's name). He is jealous of the progress with which Allah (to whom praises are due) is blessing me and my followers, and this jealousy is about to run Mr. Dawud insane. (*The Crusader* erroneously called him an Imam.) Mr. Dawud and Miss Staton should have been ashamed to try to make fun of me and my followers while publicly serving the devil in the theatrical world. I do not allow my followers to visit such, nor do I allow my wife and the believing women who follow me to go before the public partly dressed. If they would, never would I claim them to be mine any more.
>
> (Muhammad, "Mr. Muhammad Speaks," 15 August 1959, 14)

At no time did Elijah Muhammad engage in a serious discussion of the accusations made by Dawud.

Jamil Daib, a Palestinian Arab who came to the United States in 1948, was unusual in that he once had close ties with the Nation of Islam. He had served as the principal of Elijah Muhammad's University of Islam in Chicago, but was fired for teaching a more traditional formulation of Islam. Daib later described the Nation of Islam as a cult with no resemblance to Islam: "They have different religious books, prayers, their fasts, in fact the criteria by which Muslims and non-Muslims judge an organization or group to be an Islamic one – cannot be applied to this group" ("Fire New Blasts at Moslems," 1–2). For him, one of the hallmarks of Islam is universal brotherhood, which the Nation of Islam clearly opposed. He declared that the movement was not part of Islam.

Daib's questionable assertion that Islam was race-blind, and notwithstanding the other accusations about deviations from orthodoxy and orthopraxis, such as those made by Dawud, was left unaddressed except by ad hominem attacks. Later, others such as the Ahmadiyya Adib Nurud-din, in 1962, also dismissed Elijah Muhammad's teachings as absurd. A decade later an Ahmadiyya Muslim also criticized Elijah Muhammad and the Nation of Islam. *Muhammad Speaks* responded by claiming that the Ahmadi movement originated in British India and was financed by Christians to help pacify Muslims who were revolting against British rule. Ironically, given that Elijah Muhammad depended on an Ahmadiyya translation of the Qur'an, the article asserted that: "The movement tailored the Holy Quran to meet the needs and objectives of the foreign occupier" (Baghdadi, 2). Elijah Muhammad may have relied heavily on personal attacks because these Muslim critics had centuries of traditional Islamic doctrine on their side. In many cases they knew the Qur'an better than he, and no doubt surpassed his knowledge of the Sunna and the sira. And his usual trump card, his unique access to Allah, held no value with these opponents.

"COPPER-COLORED" BROTHERS

Elijah Muhammad had support from some non-Nation of Islam Muslims in the United States. The most notable was Abdul Basit Naeem, a Pakistani author who regularly contributed to *Muhammad Speaks*. He minimized the differences between Elijah Muhammad's Islam and those of other Muslims; these differences did not affect the essence of Islam, and besides, the end justified the means. His followers in the Nation of Islam studied the Qur'an and performed the prayers. When criticism came from Muslims outside the United States, often referred to as Muslims from the East or Orthodox Muslims, Naeem encouraged Elijah Muhammad to ignore their suggestions, particularly in matters that were essentially local; the Muslims from the East were ignorant of the burden he had in resurrecting the "mentally dead" who still languished under the devil's rule.

In the first two decades of the Nation of Islam, Elijah Muhammad seems to have had no issues with Eastern Muslims. By the late 1950s, he still had only two critiques. First, he thought that the Arab Muslims' efforts to convert whites to Islam were pointless. Second, he was also concerned that scholars of the Qur'an overemphasized Allah as "spirit" in the same way that Christians did. He also recognized that his goals were not identical to those of other Muslims. The goals of "Islam in America" were to teach African Americans the "truth," that is, to teach them self-respect and unity, to bring them face to face with Allah, and to reject white devils. Initially, he probably assumed that these goals were compatible – probably even identical – with the Islams of other Muslims. Perhaps because of early interactions with Muslims from the East, such as Naeem, he assumed that all Muslims would accept him and his teachings.

In *The Supreme Wisdom* Elijah Muhammad clearly still had a utopian image of Muslims in the East. These Muslims had no slavery, they lived in peace as true brothers and sisters to each other in the best and richest part of the world. Rather naively, he expected that any of his followers would be "welcomed with sincere and open arms and recognized by his light-skinned or copper-colored Arab brother" (Muhammad, *The Supreme Wisdom*, 37). When Malcolm X was sent in 1959 to arrange the travel details for Elijah Muhammad's subsequent trip to the Middle East, he confirmed his mentor's idyllic image of the Muslims of the region. He wrote that Arabs came in "many different shades, ranging from regal black to rich brown, but none are white." He added that Arabs see African Americans as "our brothers of color" and that there "is no color prejudice among the Moslems" (X, "Arabs Send Warm Greetings," 1).

Elijah Muhammad was soon disabused of these misconceptions by his own travels within the Muslim world. But for the time being, he simply sought to minimize religious differences. At the same time, he made a few superficial concessions, including going on pilgrimage to burnish his Islamic credentials. He considered "Eastern Muslims" as merely conservative or confused:

> My brothers in the East were never subjected to conditions of slavery and systematic brainwashing by the slavemasters for as long a period of time as my people here were subjected. I cannot, therefore, blame them if they differ with me in certain interpretations of the Message of Islam. In fact, I do not even *expect* them to understand some of the things I say unto my people here.
>
> (Naeem, "Introduction" to Muhammad, *The Supreme Wisdom*, 4)

He tried to explain the unique circumstances in which he and other African Americans found themselves, and why, for example, they prayed in English and not Arabic. They had lost their original language and homeland when they were forcibly taken from Africa as slaves. As a result, the Nation of Islam had no choice but to worship Allah in English; he added that, in any case, Allah hears prayers regardless of the language in which they are offered.

According to Claude Andrew Clegg III, Elijah Muhammad's *'umra* had two additional effects. Perhaps a bit superficially, Elijah Muhammad was willing to align his formulation of Islam with those of other Muslims by, for example, renaming his temples "mosques." The greater impact was his disappointment in "the East": instead of opulent wealth, he found poverty; instead of a society of brilliant scientists, he found pre-modern societies. Clegg argues that Elijah Muhammad's disappointment with the Middle East caused him to de-emphasize the importance of making overtures to Arab and African Muslims and to stress traditional elements of the Nation of Islam's doctrines. To a large degree, he lost respect for those he had esteemed as the Tribe of Shabazz in East Asia ... Interestingly, the Afro-Asian tour had afforded him credibility and validation, but it also instilled in him a measure of disillusionment that reinforced the very beliefs and practices for which orthodox Muslims had scorned him (Clegg, 144).

Although Elijah Muhammad was always willing to confront Muslims who questioned his orthodoxy, in 1963 he rather idealistically still held hope for a rapprochement. He minimized the disagreements between himself and Eastern Muslims and insisted that they were not enemies.

And yet, his willingness to oppose these other Muslims was increasing. In the same article in which he declared "we are not enemies," he suggested that these Eastern Muslims were gradually coming to agree with him about the nature of the devils. Somewhat more stridently, he insisted that, "It is in the Holy Qur-an that these people are the devils, and the scholars of Islam know it." Ultimately, Elijah Muhammad drew his authority not from the Qur'an, but from his commission from Allah in the person of Fard Muhammad. Relying solely on the Qur'an would have been a poor tactic. From his travels he must have been aware that many of his learned Eastern Muslim interlocutors knew the Qur'an far more thoroughly than he. For him and his followers, nothing and no one could trump the authority of Allah: "I am sent from Allah and not from the Secretary General of the Muslim League. There is no Muslim in Arabia that has authority to stop me from delivering this message that I have been assigned to by Allah ... I am not taking orders from them, I am taking orders from Allah (God) himself" (Muhammad, "Mr. Muhammad Answers Critics," 3–4). It was just a matter of time, therefore, before he would break with his Eastern co-religionists.

WHITE MUSLIMS

Elijah Muhammad was quite willing to criticize and castigate anyone who opposed him. It is a sign of the centrality of Islam (as he understood it) to his identity that he took criticisms from other Muslims so seriously. From the mid-1960s onward, well after his travels to the Middle East but about the same time that Malcolm X and his sons Wallace and Akbar Muhammad broke with his formulation of Islam, he became increasingly hostile. For the first time, he recognized the threat represented by the other Islam of these Eastern Muslims. (Their Islam, of course, would be best described as "Islams," but Elijah Muhammad seems to have been unaware of the diversity within Islam. Even the differences between Sunnis and Shi'is were never mentioned by him.) He increasingly came to see these Muslims, who seemed only interested in criticizing him, as corrupted and even as hypocrites. By the 1970s, he used stronger language, criticizing "old-world" Muslims for following an "old Islam led by Whites" and claiming that they were no better than white Christians.

Along with Elijah Muhammad's recognition of the threat posed by "orthodox" Islam, came the recognition that these Muslims were not coming gradually to agree with him. In 1965 he introduced a dichotomy into Islam, his new Islam was displacing their old Islam:

> The Orthodox Muslims will have to bow to the choice of Allah. Allah will bring about a new Islam. As for the Principles of Belief, they remain the same … We are seeing this change now and entering into it. The devils oppose this change, and the Orthodox join them in opposing us because of their desire to carry on the old way of Islam.
>
> (Muhammad, *Message*, 49–50)

Earlier, he had assumed that Muslims of the East recognized the truth of his reading of the Qur'an, but they kept it hidden.

Now he took a new tack; they no longer understood their own scripture:

> Many Orthodox Muslims do not want to believe that Allah has appeared in the Person of Master Fard Muhammad or that He has made manifest the truth that has been hidden from their religious scientists – the truth of God and of the devil as revealed to me. Though they do have the Holy Qur-an, many of them do not understand the meaning of it, and some of them believe everything that is prophesied in the Bible and Holy Qur-an about a last Messenger or Prophet being or referring to Muhammad of 1,400 years ago.
>
> (Muhammad, *Message*, 187)

This is the same period in which he began to make the argument that he was the prophet referred to in the prayer of Abraham; he, not Muhammad, had been sent to a people who had no other prophet, and African Americans were a community that needed their own messenger who speaks their language. In other words, he began to use the Qur'an to attack Orthodox Muslims. His new defensiveness was not just about his claim to be a messenger of Allah, but about the very nature of Allah himself – which was the most contentious issue for non-Nation of Islam Muslims:

> Some Orthodox Muslims mock us for the sake of being accepted as a friend of their and our enemy. They are spooky minded and believe that Allah (God) is some immaterial something … The ignorant belief of the Orthodox Muslims, that Allah (God) is Some Formless Something and yet He Has An Interest in our affairs, can be condemned in no limit of time. I would not give two cents for that kind of God, in which they believe.
>
> (Muhammad, "Black Man of U.S.A. and Africa," 20)

It should be noted that at this point, the mid-1960s, Elijah Muhammad merely felt that his Muslim detractors were religiously confused and mistakenly befriending the devil. Thus far he had avoided his favorite argument, the ad hominem. For Eastern Muslims at least, he opted to address directly the main critiques of his teachings: his claim to be a prophet and his claim that Fard Muhammad was Allah.

Only in the 1970s did Elijah Muhammad make a definitive break with his co-religionist opponents. This break came with his declaration that other Muslims not only were seeking to befriend the "white devils" and were confused about the true teachings of the Qur'an and Islam, but also were themselves "white." Elijah Muhammad wrote: "We have a New Islam coming up. The Old Islam was led by white people, white Muslims, but this one will not be. This Islam will be established and led by Black Muslims only" ("Allah's Last Messenger Answers Questions You Have Always Wanted to Ask!" 4). The once "copper-colored" Muslims of the East had become "white" Muslims. Their Islam was no better than the devils' Christianity: "The Christians and most old world Muslims are alike: not having a true knowledge of the Supreme One, referred to as Allah, and God makes most people believe that God is something other than a man" (Muhammad, *Our Saviour Has Arrived*, 61). Yet, even as late as 1973 he held out some hope: "We are bringing you a New Islam. White people tell Me sometimes, 'Those Orthodox Muslims over there do not believe in Your teachings.' I say, 'Well that is natural. This is something new which they never heard before. It takes time'" (Muhammad, *Theology of Time*, 83).

For Elijah Muhammad, the claim to be Allah's Apostle did not depend on recognition by Orthodox, old world, Muslims of the East – even though he initially sought some legitimacy from them. He had been "missioned" by Allah himself: "It is impossible for one to believe in either One – God or the Messenger – and not believe in Both, for the Messenger is the only source of communication and guidance for the people. So, rejecting the Messenger is rejecting God, The Sender of the Messenger"

(Muhammad, "The Hypocrites," 12). Thus, to reject him as the Apostle, or to reject Allah as he knew him in Fard Muhammad, was to reject Islam. Mutual ignorance allowed him and some non-Nation of Islam Muslims to assume that their differences could be resolved. After all, there were many variations in Islam. However, as that ignorance was gradually eliminated by familiarity, the incompatibility of their formulations of Islam became increasingly obvious. In a testament to the firmness of his convictions, when that incompatibility led to a sustained criticism, he abandoned (in fits and starts) his earlier appeal to Muslims from the East in favor of complete rejection of them. His black Islam was the new and true Islam.

ISLAMIC TRAJECTORIES

In 1933 Elijah Muhammad's seventh son, Warith Deen Mohammed, originally Wallace D. Muhammad, was born. He was the last of his children to be born during Fard Muhammad's presence. That same year Louis Farrakhan, originally Louis Eugene Walcott, was born. Both men were profoundly influenced by Elijah Muhammad and, after his death, both claimed to be continuing his mission. Wallace Muhammad's life represents the forces in the Nation of Islam, in many ways encouraged by Elijah Muhammad himself, that pushed the movement toward a formulation of Islam that resembled that of "Orthodox Muslims." Many others, including Malcolm X, had had similar impulses, but they did so by leaving the Nation of Islam. Wallace D. Muhammad not so: although he was repeatedly expelled, he kept returning to his father's movement. In 1975 on Saviour's Day, 26 February, just one day after his father had died, he was acclaimed as the new supreme minister of the Nation of Islam. Almost immediately he began systematically to dismantle the movement that his father had spent forty years building and defending. Louis Farrakhan initially acknowledged Wallace D. Muhammad as his new leader. Farrakhan's meteoric rise in the Nation of Islam after the fall of Malcolm X made him the logical successor to Elijah Muhammad in the eyes of many in the Nation of Islam. Two years after Wallace Muhammad began the task of bringing the Nation of Islam into harmony with Sunni Islam, Louis Farrakhan broke with him, and began the "second resurrection" of the Nation of Islam. Thus Farrakhan's life represents the traditional, conservative forces in the Nation of Islam for whom race trumped any other orthodox trends.

Warith Deen Mohammed

Wallace D. Muhammad had had little contact with his father during his years of hiding and imprisonment, that is from his birth in 1933 to his father's release from prison in 1946. His formal education may have occurred entirely within the University of Islam, but during that period he was also exposed to Sunni Islam from his teachers of Arabic and Islam, who included the aforementioned Jamil Diab, who later became a harsh critic of Wallace Muhammad's father. As a young man, he began to doubt some of the teachings of his father. He had also noted that, in the famous oil painting of Fard Muhammad that Elijah Muhammad kept in his house, the founder of this black Islamic movement looked very much like a white man. By Wallace Muhammad's mid-twenties, many in the Nation of Islam saw him as his father's successor. In 1961 he was convicted of draft-dodging, like his father, and served his three-year sentence in a federal penitentiary. His objection to military service seems to have been out of principle, for he opted for the prison sentence over community service because he felt the latter would still aid the war effort in Vietnam.

Wallace Muhammad had raised his doctrinal doubts with his father just prior to imprisonment, and during his incarceration he had time to study the Qur'an in great depth. Despite the growing suspicion of the racial teachings of his father, he resumed his position as a minister upon his release. When he first broke with his father, it had as much to do with the events surrounding Malcolm X as doctrinal disagreements with his father. It was he who confirmed the rumors of infidelity and illegitimate children to Malcolm X, and it was they two who sought biblical and qur'anic precedents to justify them. According to Malcolm X, Wallace Muhammad had also tried to convince him that "the only possible solution for the Nation of Islam would be its accepting and projecting a better understanding of Orthodox Islam" (X and Haley, 339). For his loyalty to Malcolm X and his role in this scandal, Wallace Muhammad was suspended from the movement in 1964 and cut off from financial support. Shortly after Malcolm X's assassination, he publicly humbled himself before his father and was reinstated. His views on Islam had not changed, however, and he was later suspended at least two more times because of his doctrinal deviance from his father's teaching on Fard Muhammad and Allah. He was reinstated in 1969 and again in 1971, but only in 1974 did he regain his position as a minister in the Nation of Islam. Wallace Muhammad would later claim that, after having been accepted back this final time by his father in 1974, he had given him permission to teach his understanding of Islam, that is, to move the Nation of Islam toward Sunni Islam by abandoning its racialist teachings. Elijah Muhammad is quoted as saying, "My son's got it, my son can go anywhere on earth and preach" (Marsh, 91).

Wallace Muhammad's succession was not as clean or preordained as he claimed it to be. Just prior to Elijah Muhammad's death in 1975, *Muhammad Speaks* was highlighting the many prominent members of the Nation of Islam, particularly Wallace

Muhammad and Louis Farrakhan. Although the latter was related by marriage, the Muhammad family wanted to keep the leadership within the family. The six-person council that nominated him contained only one non-family member: Muhammad Ali. Wallace Muhammad eventually secured the support of Louis Farrakhan, Raymond Sharrieff, and two of his own brothers. The Saviour's Day rally saw these key members publicly pledge allegiance to him – though it should be noted that the two men who later broke with him, Louis Farrakhan and Raymond Sharrieff, both pledged to continue in the tradition of Elijah Muhammad and did not pledge allegiance to Wallace Muhammad himself. The cover of the next *Muhammad Speaks* had two pictures of Wallace Muhammad within a picture of Elijah Muhammad, which also officially announced the latter's death. These pictures included the famous picture of a seated Elijah Muhammad with Wallace Muhammad standing beside him with his hand on his father's shoulder (with the oil painting of Fard Muhammad behind them and the Qur'an in front of them). To make the message explicit, the heading "Muslim Ministers Declare Support For New Leadership" appeared over the pictures of the top officials of the Nation of Islam and family members, including Yusuf Shah, Nathaniel Muhammad, Abass Rassoull, Raymond Sharrieff, Muhammad Ali, Abdul Karriem, Abdul Rahman, Jeremiah Shabazz, and, of course, Louis Farrakhan. No hint of the internal political struggle or the tentative pledges by some officials who disliked his doctrinal deviancy was provided. Wallace Muhammad, for his part, certainly played up the prophecy angle, even though he came to reject almost every element on which it was based; when asked why he was his father's successor rather than one of his elder brothers, he said:

> My personal answer would be it was God's intention. It was God's plan. But I have also heard my Father, Himself, say that

> when I was born or I was conceived in my mother, He had been born as the Servant, the Messenger of God, who manifested Himself with W.F. Muhammad; and by me being born at the time when He was in contact with His Savior, the God in Person, helped to form me, not only as a child of His loins, but a child for the Mission … [T]here was never any doubt in His mind that I would be the one who would come to this office.
>
> ("First Official Interview," 3)

In the same interview, Wallace Muhammad also related that his mother and father had been told by Fard Muhammad himself that Wallace Muhammad would be born a boy and would be "a helper to his father."

As the Nation of Islam's new supreme minister, Wallace Muhammad dismantled the organization financially (out of necessity) and doctrinally (out of conviction). Despite being worth forty-six million dollars (thirty million dollars less than had been thought), the Nation of Islam had millions of dollars of debt. Wallace Muhammad sold off businesses to pay creditors and taxes. More significantly, he began to shift the racial emphasis of the teachings of his father by, for example, no longer calling Caucasians "devils," but by speaking of the mindset that had dominated them as "devilish." The demand for a separate state for African Americans, and anti-American and anti-Christian slogans, were simply dropped. Wallace Muhammad had inherited Fard Muhammad's penchant for renaming. The nationality of his followers was changed from the tribe of Shabazz to Bilalians, since Bilal was an African slave in Mecca who converted to Islam in the time of Muhammad. Of course, this identification with a Companion of Muhammad was also unusual, and was later dropped. Fard Muhammad was spoken of as a "wise man" and his father as "Master" as opposed to Allah in person and his apostle or messenger. Wallace Muhammad did not even spare himself from this process; his role was certainly not that of messenger but of the much more acceptable "*mujeddid*" (a reviver of Islam); the "Supreme Minister of the Nation of Islam, the Honorable Wallace D. Muhammad" became "Imam Warith Deen Mohammed" – with the change in spelling of "Muhammad" meant to emphasize an intentional break with his father's claim to be a messenger; and the Nation of Islam was first renamed the World Community of al-Islam in the West and, later, changed to the American Muslim Mission. The latter was increasingly run not by Warith Deen Mohammed, but by a council, a *shura*. Even the Universities of Islam were renamed, becoming Sister Clara Muhammad Schools in honor of his mother. Within a few years of the death of the Nation of Islam's founder, the Nation of Islam was dead – at least until its "second resurrection" under Louis Farrakhan.

Warith Deen Mohammed's most intriguing innovation, however, was his reinterpretation of the Nation of Islam's origin, its *raison d'être*. This innovation permitted him to incorporate his father's mythology, though at the same time reject it, thereby making the religious journey of his followers from the Nation of Islam to Islam meaningful and purposeful. He claimed that the movement's transition to "orthodoxy" had been Fard Muhammad's plan from the beginning. That is to say, Fard Muhammad had consciously, though secretly, sowed the seeds for the Nation of Islam's own demise in favor of Sunni Islam. In the decade before Warith Deen Mohammed's death in 2008, he portrayed Fard Muhammad as someone whose true but secret purpose was to bring African Americans to "orthodox Islam." However, they were unprepared even to study the Qur'an, for they knew no Arabic and did not even recognize its authority. He taught that Fard Muhammad had instructed Elijah Muhammad that: "When the time comes your children will learn the Qur'an, and they will teach you." Simply introducing the Qur'an was sufficient, for it would eventually prompt

Muslims toward orthodox Islam – as it had with Warith Deen Mohammed. To facilitate that inevitable shift, Fard Muhammad first had to establish the Nation of Islam "as a strategy, a temporary strategy, a temporary language environment, to hold uneducated Blacks … long enough to come into an independent mind … and then later study the Qur'an." In fact, according to Warith Deen Mohammed, Fard Muhammad knew that things would get better in America for African Americans. Eventually, as they would become more educated, they would question the very racial myth that Fard Muhammad had created. They would discover that Fard Muhammad himself had sowed the seeds of its own destruction and had even ridiculed it by teaching, first, that whites were evil though a black man had created them, and second, that Allah was the son of a black man and a white woman.

Warith Deen Mohammed's most important piece of evidence for his mythic revision was the predicted future book. As he told the story, Fard Muhammad had taught Elijah Muhammad that "there is coming another Islam. You will get another holy Qur'an." When Fard Muhammad gave his future successor an Arabic book, Elijah Muhammad initially understood it to be that new Qur'an, the future book. For years he kept it wrapped in its green cover, stored in a place of honor. After his sons Akbar and Wallace Muhammad had studied Arabic, he had them read it to him. To the surprise of all, it turned out to be an Arabic Qur'an, no different than any other Qur'an. Warith Deen Mohammed understood this event to confirm Fard Muhammad's secret plan for African Americans to "choose the Islam that is in the Qur'an." Though Fard Muhammad had wanted to promulgate Islam, establishing independent thinking was a prerequisite. As for Elijah Muhammad, even he acknowledged the plan at the very end of his life. By appointing as his successor Wallace Muhammad, whom he had expelled several times for his orthodox Sunni proclivities, he demonstrated that he too now recognized Fard Muhammad's secret plan (Mohammed, "Address to the University of North Carolina at Wilmington"). This mythic revision by Warith Deen Mohammed, however, is hard to reconcile with his father's own claims. First, Elijah Muhammad was aware that the books that he had been given by Fard Muhammad were Qur'ans: two in English and one in Arabic. Second, Elijah Muhammad stated that the future book had been written, but he had not yet received it. In 1969, long after Wallace Muhammad and Akbar Muhammad would have read this special Qur'an, Elijah Muhammad wrote, "This last Messenger is bringing it out in a book that was written by Allah (God) himself – a book that was Sealed and Kept by Allah (God). This book has not, as yet, been released" (Muhammad, "Teachings of the Holy Quran," 18). Third, the vehemence with which Elijah Muhammad taught his race myth, his hostility to Muslims who disagreed with him, and the expulsion of his own sons in the late 1960s and early 1970s for their "orthodox" beliefs seems to belie his participation in this grand ruse of Fard Muhammad. Fourth, Warith Deen Mohammed later admitted that he had not been explicitly appointed by his father.

A more plausible interpretation of Elijah Muhammad as a "proto-Muslim" comes from Edward Curtis. He suggests that Elijah Muhammad's use of the Qur'an to justify his own teachings, "elevated the status of traditional Sunni Islamic discourse, especially its sacred texts, within African-American Islamic thought" (Curtis, *Islam in Black America*, 18–19). Ultimately, employing the Qur'an in this fashion for so many decades created an authority for the Qur'an, which handed the advantage to his non-Nation of Islam Muslim opponents whose facility with the Qur'an so outweighed his own. After all, it was the reading of the Qur'an and the influence of those opponents that drove a wedge between him and his own sons, Akbar and Wallace, and his first protégé, Malcolm X. One could argue, therefore, that Elijah Muhammad's own emphasis on the Qur'an, and even his constant exegesis of it, made the shift to a more familiar formulation of Islam inevitable, though quite unpremeditated. Thus Warith Deen Mohammed's elaborate re-envisioned myth of origins is not necessary. The transition to the "Islam of the Qur'an" occurred not because of the alleged secret ends of Fard Muhammad, but because of the means that Elijah Muhammad had used to achieve his other explicit ends.

Warith Deen Mohammed's myth of origins for the Nation of Islam, however, served a very useful function for himself and his own followers. All of the first members of his organization came to Islam via the Nation of Islam. For decades they thought of Fard Muhammad as Allah and Elijah Muhammad as his messenger. The story of Fard Muhammad's secret plan, as constructed by Warith Deen Mohammed, made it possible to understand their earlier "un-Islamic" beliefs as a prerequisite stage. It reflected their own journeys, validating who they once had been and declaring as inevitable who they became. In that sense it was like Elijah Muhammad's racial mythology. It put the past and the present within a prophesied (and therefore meaningful) plan. Warith Deen Mohammed was convinced that just prior to Elijah Muhammad's death even his father had privately rejected his own teaching that Fard Muhammad was Allah and that he was his messenger. In other words, Elijah Muhammad died an "orthodox" Sunni Muslim.

Louis Farrakhan

Another way to understand the religious changes initiated by Warith Deen Mohammed is to examine the socio-economic changes of members of the Nation of Islam. Lawrence Mamiya has suggested that Elijah Muhammad's social and economic programs were remarkably successful. By the mid-1970s the socio-economic status of many members of the Nation of Islam had improved dramatically. The "black particularism" ideology that had drawn these lower-class members to the movement was no longer appropriate for their new middle-class lives. For them, Warith Deen Mohammed's transformation to "universalist" Islam came at the right time for many members of the Nation of Islam: middle-class African Americans did not need or want the strict discipline, the racial barriers, and the alienation from mainstream American political, social, and economic life (Mamiya, 138–152). Most African Americans had not made this progress, however, and still suffered the same moral, social, and economic ills that had made Elijah Muhammad's original message so potent. The formulation of Islam proffered by Warith Deen Mohammed lacked the same transformative power. Moreover, with such a radical and hasty transformation of Elijah Muhammad's teachings and movement, it was inevitable that many conservative members of the Nation of Islam would balk at them. Their Islam was one in which Elijah Muhammad and his racial teachings were essential. It was Louis Farrakhan who came to represent this conservative element. He initially supported Warith Deen Mohammed only very grudgingly, and his misgivings about Elijah Muhammad's son's commitment to his father's original teachings proved true. So in 1977 he re-established the Nation of Islam with Elijah Muhammad's original teachings.

Louis Farrakhan had been one of the more educated leaders within the Nation of Islam, having earned a high-school diploma and studied for two years at a teachers' college. He had been a professional violinist and calypso singer. When Elijah Muhammad ordered all musicians in the Nation of Islam to give up music, Louis X (as he was then named) dutifully obeyed, despite having joined the movement just weeks earlier. Later, his musical talent would be used on behalf of the Nation of Islam when he wrote the song, "A White Man's Heaven is a Black Man's Hell." He had been converted, as so many others, by Malcolm X and was trained by him. Minister Louis X was a similarly charismatic speaker. In 1964 he broke with Malcolm X and is said to have been among those who reported to Elijah Muhammad that Malcolm X was spreading rumors about the leader's adulterous activities. When Malcolm X was later expelled, it was Louis X who most publicly and viciously attacked Malcolm X, his former mentor.

Louis X quickly filled the vacuum left by Malcolm X, becoming the minister of Temple No. 7 in New York City and being appointed the national spokesman, whose duties included introducing Elijah Muhammad at the annual Saviour's Day rallies, just as Malcolm X had done. Elijah Muhammad replaced his "X" with "Farrakhan" in the late 1960s as a sign of his new protégé's ascension within the Nation of Islam.

Despite Farrakhan's public fealty to Wallace Muhammad after his father's death, he was still viewed as a threat to the new leader. In Wallace Muhammad's first interview he was asked about Louis Farrakhan specifically, "We understand he had pledged his allegiance to you just as he did to your Father before you, along with the other ministers of the Nation. Do you feel that you can depend on their loyalty if outside influences and inside influences try to bring about a split in the Nation of Islam?" Wallace Muhammad replied, "Their pledges of allegiance were received in all sincerity. I have nothing to say that would reflect anything else. One correction here: The title of Minister Louis Farrakhan is National Representative of the Supreme Minister" ("First Official Interview," 12). Farrakhan served as Wallace Muhammad's international spokesman until December 1977, when he announced his departure from the newly Sunni movement. He stated that he had initially been so surprised and devastated by Elijah Muhammad's death that he was reluctant to take the leadership. After two years of tolerating Warith Deen Mohammed's changes, he could no longer accept what he perceived as disrespect for Elijah Muhammad. Louis Farrakhan then reformed the Nation of Islam; it again taught that Fard Muhammad was Allah and Elijah Muhammad was his messenger, and retained the story of Mr. Yakub and his creation of the white devils, the Fall of America, and a demand for a separate territory. He also reinitiated the defunct Fruit of Islam and the Muslim Girl's Training and General Civilization Class.

Farrakhan's claims to be the true leader of the Nation of Islam seem reminiscent of Sunni–Shi'i arguments about the alleged designation of 'Ali (d. 661) by Muhammad as his successor. A month prior to Elijah Muhammad's death, two daughters of Louis Farrakhan married one of Elijah Muhammad's nephews and one of his grandsons in a double wedding. In his role as the national spokesman, many members of the Nation of Islam had seen Farrakhan as the rightful successor to Elijah Muhammad. The claim was put forth that he specifically designated Farrakhan; Elijah Muhammad is quoted as saying, "As Allah made me to take His place among the people, I am making you to … take my place." And toward the end of his life, Elijah Muhammad also said that Farrakhan was the best minister he ever had (T. Muhammad, *Chronology*, 11–12). In 1992 Abass Rassoull was still attempting to reconcile the two men in a United Nation of Islam, and he likened Farrakhan and Warith Deen Mohammed to early Christianity's Peter and Paul, respectively (Muhammad, *Theology of Time*, xli).

In over three decades since Farrakhan's resurrection of the Nation of Islam, even he has drifted from some of the teachings of Elijah Muhammad to which he had earlier clung so strongly. Like Warith Deen Mohammed he also introduced, but more gradually, more Sunni practices into his Nation of Islam. Curtis has argued that between the years 1960 and 1975 the Nation of Islam was gradually Islamized by Elijah Muhammad himself, particularly with regard to fasting. Perhaps then, both Warith Deen

Mohammed and Louis Farrakhan could be seen as merely continuing that process, but at different paces. Again, it is unlikely to have been Elijah Muhammad's intent. Rather, by adopting Islam as the Nation of Islam's religion, the Qur'an as its scripture, Allah as his deity, rituals that were very recognizably Islamic, and so forth, Elijah Muhammad created a Nation of Islam that would constantly feel the overwhelming gravitational pull of the rest of Muslim world.

CONCLUSION: THE LEGACIES

Elijah Muhammad never got his autonomous black state and the racial separation that he viewed as essential for African American survival. His enormous business empire is gone. His movement has fractured. And America has not fallen. Even his racial mythology that was so disturbingly provocative seems quaint and unthreatening now. In many ways, therefore, he would be disappointed in his own legacy. However, as C. Eric Lincoln pointed out:

> Because of him, there was a temple or mosque in a hundred cities where no mosques had existed before. There was a visible presence in the form of a hundred thousand Black Muslims – conspicuous in their frequent rallies and turnouts, and their little groceries and restaurants and bakeries and other small businesses. The clean shaven young Muslims hawking their newspapers on the streets, celebrating their rituals in prisons, debating their beliefs in the media gave to the religion of Islam a projection and a prominence undreamed of in North America.
>
> (Lincoln, "The Muslim Mission," 286)

And among those hundred thousand black Muslims stand Malcolm X, Muhammad Ali, Louis Farrakhan, and Warith Deen Mohammed. Their accomplishments are part of Elijah Muhammad's legacy. Malcolm X's influence on African Americans goes well beyond his connection to Elijah Muhammad. Certainly within popular culture and within the context of the fight for civil rights, Islam and the influence of Elijah Muhammad are all but eclipsed by his former protégé. But this does not lessen the fact that Malcolm X's iconic status would not have been possible without Elijah Muhammad. The same is true of his son Warith

Deen Mohammed. He may have changed the beliefs, practices, and even the name of his father's movement after he assumed its leadership in 1975, but there would have been no Muslim movement to change had not Elijah Muhammad toiled for four decades to build a movement that would recognize the authority of Warith Deen Mohammed and recognize that the new formulation of Islam that he espoused was related to the formulation of Islam promulgated by his father.

One does not need to reinvent Elijah Muhammad, as Warith Deen Mohammed attempted, arguing that the move of the Nation of Islam to Sunni Islam had always been part of Fard Muhammad's plan and that his father died an orthodox Sunni Muslim. Elijah Muhammad's importance to "orthodox" Islam in America does not depend on this type of revisionist history. First, despite being considered a heretic by so many other Muslims, he did what these other Muslims could not; face to face, through his ministers, and even via those who had left the Nation of Islam, Elijah Muhammad brought millions of African Americans to Islam, and Islam to the United States. Second, Elijah Muhammad's use of the Qur'an to justify his own teachings not only gave an advantage to his Muslim opponents who were far more familiar with the text, but also eventually affected key players within the Nation of Islam, most notably his own sons Akbar and Wallace, and his first protégé, Malcolm X. Thus, Elijah Muhammad's own profound attachment to Islam and its scripture made the eventual shift away from his racial formulation of Islam almost inevitable.

To look solely at what his movement became under the leadership of his son is also to miss many other aspects of the legacy. The race mythology should not be dismissed as a mere oddity or heresy. It reversed the traditional (and equally racial, even racist) accounts of the European and African contributions to civilization. Thus the myth, or at least its implications, could become a source of pride, inspiration, and revolutionary ideas to African Americans. Many white Americans certainly matched its description of whites as uncivilized racists. Perhaps most importantly, it forcefully declared the centuries of slavery and decades of lynchings, discrimination, and systematic humiliation as aberrations from an ideal. It was not the fault of African Americans. They were not somehow lesser human beings who deserved or who had permitted such atrocities to take place. They were in fact an ancient, proud, dignified people who had been subjected to evil. For example, the theodicy most often employed by Elijah Muhammad to explain why the devils were permitted to make slaves of African Americans' "innocent, Righteous forefathers in Africa" is "Allah, our God, has revealed to us that it was all for a Divine Purpose – to fulfill the prophecies of the Scriptures" (Muhammad, *The Supreme Wisdom: Volume Two*, backcover). To return to the ideal, that is, the greatness that was rightly theirs, African Americans must return to (the Nation of) Islam. The story of ancient black humanity, Mr. Yakub, and the six-thousand-year white rule employs a tactic that many myths use: it creates a pristine moment in the past and brackets out the intervening and recent history as a failure to maintain that purity. Thus it gave hope that change was not only possible, but inevitable. And all the economic, social, and political programs of Elijah Muhammad that other Muslims might find problematic, provided practical means to achieve that change.

Islam too is important to this racial mythology. The story of the Tribe of Shabazz, of the grafting of the white race, of the enslavement of blacks in America by whites, and of the Fall of America, have no close parallel in other formulations of Islam. Thus, the whole mythology could have been told without reference to the Bible or the Qur'an. There is little evidence to suggest that Fard Muhammad systematically employed these scriptures in the creation of this myth. Elijah Muhammad, however, did. He reinterpreted individual biblical and qur'anic passages (and sometimes their myths) to fit, substantiate, and elaborate his myth. This is particularly evident in the depictions of Moses, Jesus, and Muhammad, whose traditional biographies are ignored and for whom new roles are created within Elijah Muhammad's Islam. In this he was following the path trodden by many of the ghulat. By so doing, he was also able to do something that Muslim missionaries had largely failed to do: break the bonds many African Americans had to Christianity. Through his use of scripture, he undermined Christianity, the religion from which his converts came, not as being unnatural for African Americans (as Drew Ali had done) but as an evil, enslaving religion created by the white devils. He read the Bible largely as a secret, allegorical text that, if decoded correctly, gave the true history of the white race and prophecies of their imminent destruction. This hermeneutic, or batini reading, permitted him to employ and appeal to the one scripture with which African Americans were familiar – the Bible – and in a way that left them utterly dependent on him for its interpretation. By reading the Qur'an in much the same way, he made this then unknown text into scripture. It also helped him forge a new Islamic identity for his followers and a new Islamic authority for himself that would come to supersede the Christian identity, scripture, and religious authorities of African Americans that kept them mentally enslaved to the "white devil."

For Elijah Muhammad, a scripture's authority came largely from the historical and prophetic truths it contained. His role as messenger was to discover and propagate these truths. And in this way prophetic scripture, specifically the passages of the Bible or the Qur'an that he felt addressed his race myth and eschatology, demonstrated that he was the Messenger of Allah. But in so doing, he sowed the seeds of the independent authority of Islam and the Qur'an, which would rapidly come to the fore once he had died. Although Wallace Muhammad inherited his authority, he had long ago acknowledged the Qur'an as the true authority in Islam. His father's claim to absolute authority as the Messenger of Allah went with him to the grave. Wallace Muhammad made only half-hearted attempts to retain that charismatic authority by making claims to have been anointed by Elijah Muhammad and prophesied by Fard Muhammad. He handed over the authority to determine doctrinal orthodoxy to the Qur'an. Texts do not speak for themselves of course; they must be interpreted. Therefore, in reality Warith Deen Mohammed handed over doctrinal matters to formulations of Islam that he believed to be "orthodox" – in his case Sunni Islam, though he preferred the term "the Islam of the Qur'an."

The Qur'an for Elijah Muhammad was the core of the new Muslim identity that he was hoping to forge, whereas for Drew Ali it (or rather the *Koran* he cobbled together from non-qur'anic sources) served only to support his claim to be a prophet. The Qur'an, as Elijah Muhammad taught, was the scripture of the original black humanity and Islam the only appropriate religion for African Americans. It was central, but the Qur'an was never meant to be ultimate authority: he gave primacy to the racial teachings that he had received directly from Allah, in the person of Fard Muhammad. In the end, however, despite his belief that the authority of the Qur'an would be superseded by a new scripture, it was his own authority and that of the racial myth that would give way to a far more traditional interpretation of Islam, one that made the Qur'an the highest authority.

Elijah Muhammad was not the first to teach Islam in the United States. Nor did he do so in a vacuum. Islam had been associated with Africa and as an opponent of European and American Christianity. This association made Islam a natural ally of the racial mythology that he and Fard Muhammad promulgated. Drew Ali had already introduced the notion that the true identity of African Americans is Muslim and that their scripture was called the "Koran." Ahmadiyya missionaries had had limited success in the United States, but they had brought English literature, especially a new translation of the Qur'an with a lot of commentary built in. No doubt the success of Islam among African Americans built on these foundations, but that success is primarily due to the genius of Fard Muhammad's melding of Islam with a powerful racial mythology and the efforts of Elijah Muhammad. Together they produced a formulation of Islam that was powerfully attractive and radically transformative – as the life of Malcolm X demonstrates.

That many non-Nation of Islam Muslims, both in the United States and outside of it, decried (and continue to decry) Elijah Muhammad as a non-Muslim indicates not that he stands outside of Islam, but that he is clearly inside it, albeit at the margins. His willingness, perhaps even need, to engage these Muslim opponents in debate also demonstrates his "Muslim-ness." He was an active participant in that most traditional of Muslim debates, that is, the debate over who is a Muslim. As I have asked elsewhere (Berg, 144–146), why has his Muslim-ness been so underemphasized by scholars? It is not just that he is seen as heretical, for such assessments do not fall under the purview of scholars. Although I have focused on Elijah Muhammad as a maker of the *Muslim* world, that is, his *Islamic* legacy, his influence extends far beyond religion. His formulation of Islam included advocacy of racial separation, black nationalism, economic independence, "Black is beautiful," and even, at least in his rhetoric if not in practice, the use of violence. These all became key features of the Black Power movement of the 1960s. By focusing on these aspects of Elijah Muhammad's legacy at the expense of the Islamic ones, also allows him to join the pantheon of great African Americans, one that does not just belong to African American Muslims of the Nation of Islam. The Mr. Yakub story, the Mother Plane, his strange dietary regulations, and even his disparaging remarks about Africa are part of his formulation of Islam. Ignoring those allows one to favor the ideals of black autonomy and black values embodied by him and his movement better than any other. The figure of Elijah Muhammad's protégé Malcolm X has undergone the same reinterpretation. Malcolm X's twelve-year adherence and promulgation of Elijah Muhammad's teachings have been largely supplanted by his less than twelve months outside the Nation of Islam. Thus, he can be embraced by Sunni Muslim scholars as the paragon of acceptable African American Islam. Robin Kelley has argued:

> Malcolm X has been called many things: Pan-Africanist, father of Black Power, religious fanatic, closet conservative, incipient socialist, and a menace to society … Malcolm has become a sort of *tabula rasa*, or blank slate, on which people of different positions can write their own interpretations of his politics and legacy. Chuck D of the rap group Public Enemy and Supreme Court Justice Clarence Thomas can both declare Malcolm X their hero.
>
> (Kelley, 1233)

Even Kelley omits "Muslim." Such an omission with Elijah Muhammad's image is far more difficult than for Malcolm X's. Elijah Muhammad can be acknowledged as the "most powerful blackman in America" (as *Reader's Digest* did in the 1960s), for his contributions to the struggle against white oppression, and for the psychological, political, and economic "uplifiting" of African Americans. His novel formulation of Islam, however, cannot as easily be downplayed or even omitted. All of these acheivements were integral to that formulation *of Islam*. In that sense, he is both a maker of the Muslim world, and the maker of *a* Muslim world.

FURTHER READING

Readers intrigued by some of the issues discussed in this book or who would like alternative perspectives on Elijah Muhammad may find the following books of interest. Each book is accessible to the beginner. The texts listed here are also secondary sources and have been referred to throughout this book.

Berg, Herbert. *Elijah Muhammad and Islam*. New York: New York University Press, 2009.

Clegg III, Claude Andrew. *An Original Man: The Life and Times of Elijah Muhammad*. New York: St. Martin's Press, 1997.

Curtis, Edward E., IV. *Black Muslim Religion in the Nation of Islam, 1960–1975*. Chapel Hill: University of North Carolina Press, 2006.

Gibson, Dawn-Marie. *A Historical Analysis of the Nation of Islam, 1930–2009*. Doctoral dissertation, University of Ulster, 2009.

Jackson, Sherman A. *Islam and the Blackamerican: Looking Toward the Third Resurrection*. Oxford: Oxford University Press, 2005.

Lincoln, C. Eric. *The Black Muslims in America*. 3rd edition. Grand Rapids: Wm. B. Eerdmans, 1994 [1961].

Turner, Richard Brent. *Islam in the African-American Experience*. Bloomington and Indianapolis: Indiana University Press, 1997.

BIBLIOGRAPHY

This bibliography lists both works explicitly cited in the text and the most important sources upon which I have drawn. The titles listed in the Further Reading section are also Secondary Sources.

PRIMARY SOURCES

"Decree Akbar Muhammad." *Muhammad Speaks* (1 January 1965): 9.

Drew Ali, Noble. *The Holy Koran of the Moorish Science Temple of America*. 1927.

———*Moorish Literature*. n.d.

Federal Bureau of Investigation. "Elijah Muhammad." F.B.I. file 105-24822, http://vault.fbi.gov/elijah-muhammad.

Federal Bureau of Investigation. "Fard, Wallace D." F.B.I. files 100-33603; 100-43165; and 105-63642.

The Holy Qur-an. Ali, trans. Maulvi Muhammad, 4th rev. ed. Lahore: Ahmadiyya Anjuman Ishaat Islam, 1951.

Mohammed, Warith Deen. "Address to the University of North Carolina at Wilmington." 2 February 2002.

Muhammad, Elijah. "Beards." *Muhammad Speaks* (4 July 1969): 5.

———"Black Man of U.S.A. and Africa." *Muhammad Speaks* (17 October 1969): 20–21.

———"The Fatal Mistake." *Muhammad Speaks* (23 January 1970): 16–17.

———"From Savior's Day: The Mighty Words of the Messenger," *Muhammad Speaks* (18 March 1966): 10.

———*How to Eat to Live*. Newport News: The National Newport News and Commentator, 1967.

———"Hypocrites!" *Muhammad Speaks* (30 April 1971): 18.
———"The Hypocrites." *Muhammad Speaks* (26 April 1968): 12.
———"Indians in America." *Muhammad Speaks* (28 March 1969): 20.
———*Message to the Blackman in America*. Newport News: United Brothers Communications Systems, 1992 [1965].
———"Money Necessary." *Muhammad Speaks* (3 August 1973): 6.
———"Mr. Muhammad Answers Critics: Authority from Allah, None Other." *Muhammad Speaks* (2 August 1963): 3–4.
——— "Mr. Muhammad Speaks." *The Pittsburgh Courier* (23 July 1956): 2 (Magazine Section).
———"Mr. Muhammad Speaks." *The Pittsburgh Courier* (3 August 1957): 10.
———"Mr. Muhammad Speaks." *The Pittsburgh Courier* (15 August 1959): 14.
———"Opposition Against the Muslims," *Muhammad Speaks* (10 December 1971): 16–17.
———*Our Saviour Has Arrived*. Chicago: Muhammad's Temple of Islam No. 2, 1974.
———*The Supreme Wisdom: The Solution to the So-Called Negroes' Problem*. Newport News: The National Newport News and Commentator, 1957.
———*The Supreme Wisdom: Volume Two*. Hampton: U.B. & U.S. Communications Systems, n.d.
———"Teachings of the Holy Quran." *Muhammad Speaks* (15 August 1969): 18.
———"To the Black Woman in America." *Muhammad Speaks* (4 September 1970): 16–17.
———*The Theology of Time*. Transcribed by Abass Rassoull. Hampton: U.S. Communications Systems, 1992.
———*The True History of Master Fard Muhammad*. Comp. and ed. Nasir Makr Hakim. Atlanta: Messenger Elijah Muhammad Propagation Society, 1996.
———"Victory of the Apostle." *Muhammad Speaks* (15 January 1965): 1 and 3–4.
———"Warning to M.G.T. and G.C. Class." *Muhammad Speaks* (28 June 1968): 4.
———"Wash and Be Clean." *Muhammad Speaks* (1 August 1969): 21.
Shabazz, John. "Open Letter: Muslim Minister Writes to Malcolm." *Muhammad Speaks* (3 July 1964): 9.

X, Malcolm. "Arabs Send Warm Greetings to 'Our Brothers' of Color in U.S.A." *Pittsburgh Courier* (15 August 1959): 1 (Magazine Section).

X, Malcolm, with Alex Haley. *The Autobiography of Malcolm X*. New York: Ballantine Books, 1973 [1964].

SECONDARY SOURCES

"Allah's Last Messenger Answers Questions You Have Always Wanted to Ask! Muhammad Meets the Press!" *Muhammad Speaks* (4 February 1972): 3–4.

Austin, Allan D. *African Muslims in Antebellum America: Transatlantic Stories and Spiritual Struggles*. New York: Routledge, 1997.

Baghdadi, Ali. "Who's behind the Splinter Group? Messenger's Attackers Exposed." *Muhammad Speaks* (5 May 1972): 2.

Beynon, Erdmann Doane. "The Voodoo Cult among Negro Migrants in Detroit." *The American Journal of Sociology* 43 (July 1937–May 1938): 894–907.

Curtis, Edward E., IV. *Islam in Black America: Identity, Liberation, and Difference in African-American Islamic Thought*. Albany: State University of New York Press, 2002.

Diouf, Sylviane A. *Servants of Allah: African Muslims Enslaved in the Americas*. New York: New York University Press, 1998.

Ghareeb, Zahid Aziz al-. "Lauds Leader: Eastern Muslim Calls Nation of Islam 'Great'." *Muhammad Speaks* (2 July 1971): 15 and 18.

Essien-Udom, E. U. *Black Nationalism: A Search for an Identity in America*. New York: Dell Publishing, 1962.

"Fire New Blasts at Moslems: Leader Explains Role of 2 Groups." *Chicago Defender* (5 December 1959): 1–2.

"First Official Interview with the Supreme Minister of the Nation of Islam, The Honorable Wallace D. Muhammad." *Muhammad Speaks* (21 March 1975): 3 and 11–14.

Kelley, Robin D. G. "Malcolm X." In *Africana: The Encyclopedia of the African and African American Experience*, 1233–1236. Eds. Kwame Anthony Appiah and Henry Louis Gates, Jr. New York: Basic Civitas Books, 1999.

Lee, Martha F. *The Nation of Islam: An American Millenarian Movement*. Syracuse: Syracuse University Press, 1996.

Lincoln, Bruce. "Theses on Method." *Method & Theory in the Study of Religion*, 8.3 (1996): 225–227.

Lincoln, C. Eric. *The Black Muslims in America*. 3rd edition. Grand Rapids: Wm. B. Eerdmans, 1994 [1961].

———"The Muslim Mission in the Context of American Social History." In *African-American Religion: Interpretive Essays in History and Culture*, 279–294. Eds. Timothy E. Fulop and Albert J. Raboteau. New York: Routledge, 1997.

Mamiya, Lawrence H. "From Black Muslim to Bilalian: The Evolution of a Movement." *Journal for the Scientific Study of Religion* 21.2 (1982): 138–152.

Marr, Timothy. *The Cultural Roots of American Islamicism*. New York: Cambridge University Press, 2006.

Marsh, Clifton E. *From Black Muslims to Muslims: The Transition from Separation to Islam, 1930–1980*. Metuchen: The Scarecrow Press, 1984.

McCloud, Aminah Beverly. *African American Islam*. New York: Routledge, 1995.

"Muhammad Meets the Press!" *Muhammad Speaks* (11 February 1972): 3–4.

Muhammad, Toure. *Chronology of Nation of Islam History*. Chicago: Toure Muhammad, 1996.

Sahib, Hatim A. "The Nation of Islam." M.A. Thesis, University of Chicago, 1951.

van Ess, Josef. "Drusen und Black Muslims." *Die Welt des Islam* 14 (1973): 203–213.

INDEX

Abraham 63, 119, 128
Adam 53, 59, 79, 95
adultery, attitudes to 44
African countries and African culture 98–9
Ahmadi movement ix, 14, 123, 148
alcohol 19–20, 31, 45, 50, 77, 89, 118
Ali, John 46
Ali, Maulana Muhammad 14, 65, 72, 106, 120
Ali, Muhammad ix, 46
Ali, Yusuf 106
Allah, conceptions of 54–6
American Colonization Society 9
angels 57–8, 65
Asiatics 16, 30, 99
Atlanta, Georgia 26

"Back to Africa" programme 90
Barton, Hazel 19, 23
beliefs, Muslim 81–3
Ben Solomon, Job 8–9
Berg, Herbert (author) 148
Beynon, Erdmann Doane 20–2
The Bible 31, 52, 56, 59, 63–70, 108, 112, 116, 146
Bilal 134
Bilali, Salih 10–11
birth control 94–5
Black Islam 49–79
Black Power movement 96, 148
black pride 96–101
"Black Religion" 12
Blyden, Edward Wilmot 13
boll weevil plague 29

Canaanite Temple 14
capitalism 89–90, 101
Chicago 35–6, 116–17
Christianity 11–13, 16–20, 28–31, 38, 54, 61, 68, 89, 95, 114, 129, 146
Chuck D 149
Circle Seven Koran ix, 14–17
civil rights movement 90, 101
Clay, Cassius 46
Clegg, Claude Andrew III 96, 125
Columbus, Christopher 100
Committee of Cleanliness 100
Curtis, Edward 92, 137, 141

Daib, Jamil 122, 131
Dawud, Talib Ahmad 121–2
devils 1–2, 58, 60–3, 68, 90–7, 100, 109, 113–16, 122–9, 134, 141, 145–6; *see also* Satan
dietary restrictions 77–9, 149
"Do for self" precept 38, 87
donations 75–6, 89
Dowling, Levi H. 14, 17
Drew, Timothy ix, 14
Drew Ali, Noble ix, 11–18, 67, 90, 103, 146–8

economic self-sufficiency for African Americans 87–90
Eleventh Amendment to the United States Constitution 25
Emancipation Proclamation (1863) 25
end times 68–9
English language, use of 125
Estevan 7
eugenics 53
Evans, Clara 29; *see also* Muhammad, Clara
exegesis 109–10, 113, 138

Faisal, Daoud Ahmed 14
Fall of America 69–70, 87, 90, 141, 145
Fard, W.D. 1–2
Fard Muhammad, Wali ix, 1–6, 11–12, 18–23, 28, 30–1, 33–6, 52–7, 64, 67–72, 76–9, 95, 98, 107, 120–1, 134–8, 144–8; oil painting of 131, 133
Farr, George 18
Farrakhan, Louis x, 3, 45–8, 117, 130–5, 139–42
fasting 74–5, 105–6, 141
Federal Bureau of Investigation (FBI) x, 2, 19–20, 23, 34, 37, 40
Ford, Wallace D. 19–23, 32
Friday prayers 73
Fruit of Islam x, 40–3, 74, 141

Garvey, Marcus x, 12, 18, 87, 90
Georgia 25–6, 29
Ghalwash, Ahmad 107
ghu 6
ghuluw and the ghulat x, 5–6, 32–3, 55, 112, 146
Gibson, Dawn Marie 18
Girl's Training and General Civil-ization Class 41, 94, 141
God, belief in 56

hadiths 73, 106–9
hair, attitudes to 99–100
hajj 76–7
al-Hakim, caliph 32
Ham, son of Noah 16
Hawkins, John 110
Heaven and Hell 3, 168
How to Eat to Live 50, 77–9
hygiene 99–100
"hypocrites" formerly belonging to the Nation of Islam 116–20

Ibn Said, Umar 9–10
Ibrahim, Abd ar-Rahman 9
Islam 1–5, 8–18, 30–1, 146–7
  diversity within 50–2, 127, 130
  "old" and "new" 127, 129
  pillars of 70–7
  principles of 51–7, 86
  see also beliefs; Black Islam; Sunni Islam; wants

Jackson, Sherman A. 12
Jehovah's Witnesses 20, 69
Jesus of Nazareth 15, 17, 53, 59–64, 69, 78, 146
Jews and Judaism 60–2
Jim Crow laws 26
jinn 58
Johnson, Andrew 25–6

Ka'ba's renovation 104
Kebe, Lamine 9
Kelley, Robin 149
Kennedy, John F. 44
Khaalis, Hamaas Abdul 47
King, Martin Luther Jr. 90
The Koran *see* [The] Qur'an
Ku Klux Klan 25

Last Day, the 68
"Lesson #2" 1, 22, 55–6
Lincoln, Abraham 25
Lincoln, Bruce 51
Lincoln, C. Eric 41, 143
literacy 8
Little, Malcolm 39; *see also* X, Malcolm
lynchings x, 27–8, 145

Mahdi, use of title 32–3
Mamiya, Lawrence 138
Mary, the mother of Jesus 60
Mecca 77
Message to the Blackman in America 50, 72, 77, 87–96, 108, 113, 119–20, 127
migration 29
Million Man March 96
Milwaukee 37
Mirza Ghulam Ahmad x, 33, 112
"Mr. Muhammad Speaks" (column) 41, 49, 121–2
Moabite Temple of the World 14
Mohammed, Abdul 35
Mohammed, Warith Deen x, 3, 67–8, 130–42, 144, 147; *see also* Muhammad, Wallace D.
Moorish Science Temple of America 14–15, 18, 20, 67
Mormon teaching 100–1
Moses 53, 59–60, 66, 146
"Mother Plane" myth 69, 149
motherhood, attitudes to 94
mufassirs 108–9
Muhammad, Akbar x, 42, 45, 107, 118–19, 136–7, 144
Muhammad, Augustus 116–17
Muhammad, Bilali 10
Muhammad, Clara x, 29, 31–2, 37, 47, 107
Muhammad, Elijah x
  aliases used by 37
  allegations of adultery against 44, 140
  birth and early life of 25–30
  conservatism of 93, 96, 101
  death of 48, 133
  distinctive formulation of Islam 4–6, 11–14, 50–4, 61, 86–90, 95, 98, 101, 103, 127, 144, 148–9
  final break with orthodox Islam 129–30
  historical significance of 1, 143–4, 148–9
  illnesses of 42–3, 46–8
  imprisonent for draft-dodging 37, 87, 107
  joint interest in politics and religion 28, 30, 33, 92, 108
  marriage and family 29, 42, 133
  Muslim opposition to 36–7, 116, 120–3, 127–8, 144, 148
  "Muslim-ness" of 148
  racialist ideology of 17–18, 52, 54, 58, 61–2, 65, 68, 79, 97, 99, 108–14, 134–9, 143–8
  radicalism of 101
  relationship with Malcolm X 39, 43, 45, 117
  significance of Muhammad the Prophet for 62–3, 103–4, 119
  success as an organiser 40–2
  teachings of 49–55, 60–71, 88–97, 109
  tour to Africa and Asia 76–7, 125–6
  use made of The Qur'an 64–6, 104–14, 128, 137–8, 144–7
  view of Wali Fard Muhammad 19–24, 31–2, 35, 37, 49–50, 55–9, 68, 71–2, 89, 110–11, 115–16, 126, 129, 138, 141
  see also Message to the Blackman in America; *(The) Supreme Wisdom*
Muhammad, Elijah Jr. 42
Muhammad, Herbert (Jabir) x, 42
Muhammad, Kalot 36, 116–18
Muhammad, Lottie 42
Muhammad, Wallace D. 42, 44–5, 48, 107, 118, 131–7, 140, 144, 147; *see also* Mohammed, Warith Deen
Muhammad the Prophet 4, 17, 53, 59–64, 104, 146
Muhammad Speaks (newspaper) x, 39–48, 72, 75–7, 81, 108, 117–19, 123, 132–3
Muslim Brotherhood, American 13, 121
"Muslims from the East" 123–30
myths 145

Naeem, Abdul Basit 123–4
names, collective and individual 98
Nation of Islam 2–3, 6, 11, 21, 33, 35, 38–48, 57, 69, 74–6, 87–9, 95–6, 109, 115–18, 122–3, 130–9, 142, 145
  dark secrets of 118
  media coverage of 41–3
  renaming of 135
  setbacks for 46–7
  structure of 40–1, 48, 132–6, 141
Native Americans 8
natural disasters 69
Nimrod 60
Nurud-din, Adib 123

patriarchy 93, 95, 101
Pickthall, Marmaduke 73
pilgrimage 76–7, 125
Poole, William and Marie 26–31
pork, consumption of 78–9
prayer 71–3, 107; *see also* Friday prayers
prophecy 111–13, 133, 138
protest movements 12
Public Enemy (rap group) 96, 149

Qaddafi, Muammar 47
The Qur'an 1–2, 5, 13, 15, 52, 56–9, 63–73, 79, 146–7
  future version of 66–8, 136–7
  translations of 14, 64–5, 72–3, 106, 120, 123, 148

race riots 26
racial integration and racial separatism 26, 90–2, 134, 143
racism 11–13, 16, 28–9, 38, 99, 145
Ramadan 74, 105–6
Ramatherio, Sri 14–15
Rassoull, Abass 141
Reader's Digest 149
reincarnation doctrine 6
resurrection 68, 70
revisionist history 144
al-Risala 10
ritual 70
Rodwell, J.M. 73
Rutherford, Joseph F. 20, 69

Sadiq, Muhammad 13–14
Sahib, Hatim A. 20
Said, Edward 50–1
Satan 39, 58; *see also* devils
Saviour's Day Rally 41, 45, 48, 71, 1 33
sermons 109
sexually-transmitted diseases 93
Shabazz, tribe of xi, 53, 65, 97–8, 126, 145
shahada, the 70–1
Shari'a law 5
Sharrieff, Ethel 42
Sharrieff, Raymond xi, 42, 46, 48, 133
Sherman, William T. 25–6
shirk 54–5
"slave names" 76, 98
slavery and the slave trade 7–8, 10–12, 16, 25, 145
Staton, Dakota 121–2
Stephen the Moor 7
storytelling tradition 109–10
Sunna, the 106–7
Sunni Islam 118, 121, 131–2, 135–41, 144, 147, 149
The Supreme Wisdom 49, 66, 71–2, 90–5, 104, 110–12, 119, 124, 145

Teachings for the Lost Found Nation of Islam in a Mathematical Way 22
Thomas, Clarence 149
Turner, Henry McNeal 13

Universal Negro Improvement Assoc-iation (UNIA) 12, 18, 20, 87
University of Islam xi, 22, 35, 75, 122, 135

van Ess, Josef 32, 55
veiling of women 95

Walcott, Louis Eugene 130; *see also* Farrakhan, Louis
Wansbrough, John 109
wants, Muslim 83–6
Washington DC 37
Webb, Muhammad Alexander Russell 13
white supremacist ideology 17, 53–4, 97, 99, 101
Wilmington, North Carolina 26
women
  protection and restriction of 93–9
  role and status of 94–5

X, Louis 45, 117, 139–40; *see also* Farrakhan, Louis
X, Malcolm xi, 3, 28, 38–45, 71, 93, 117–18, 124, 130, 132, 137–40, 143–4, 148–9
"X" names in general 76, 98

Yakub xi, 2, 52–5, 58–9, 62, 66, 94, 97, 111, 141, 145, 149